IN
WISDOM
&
ORDER

IN WISDOM & ORDER

~BOYD K.~
PACKER

DESERET
BOOK

SALT LAKE CITY, UTAH

© 2013 Boyd K. Packer

All rights reserved. No part of this book may be reproduced in any form or by any means without permission in writing from the publisher, Deseret Book Company, at permissions @deseretbook.com or P. O. Box 30178, Salt Lake City, Utah 84130. This work is not an official publication of The Church of Jesus Christ of Latter-day Saints. The views expressed herein are the responsibility of the author and do not necessarily represent the position of the Church or of Deseret Book Company.

DESERET BOOK is a registered trademark of Deseret Book Company.

Visit us at DeseretBook.com

Library of Congress Cataloging-in-Publication Data

CIP data on file
ISBN 978-1-60907-852-2

Printed in the United States of America
Publishers Printing, Salt Lake City, UT

10   9   8   7   6   5   4   3   2   1

See that all these things are done

in wisdom and order;

for it is not requisite that a man

should run faster than he has strength.

And again, it is expedient

that he should be diligent,

that thereby he might win the prize;

therefore, all things

must be done in order.

MOSIAH 4:27

CONTENTS

CONTENTS

PART ONE

GOSPEL FOUNDATIONS

1

FAITH

During World War II the city of Osaka, Japan, was almost obliterated. Her buildings were rubble, and her streets were littered with blocks, debris, and bomb craters. The subway had been protected, and soon after the occupation, it became the only means of transportation for the city.

One beautiful day in late fall several servicemen and I came up the steps from the subway. As far as we could see lay the desolation of war.

What had been a broad thoroughfare lined with sycamore trees was now a scene of hopeless destruction. Although most of the trees had been blasted completely away, some few of them still stood with shattered limbs and trunks. One or two of them had gathered the courage to send out a few new shoots and had produced a meager crop of foliage. A gentle breeze was scattering the yellow leaves among the debris.

A tiny Japanese girl in a tattered kimono was busily climbing over the rubble, gathering the sycamore leaves into a bouquet. The little

---

From an address given at general conference, October 1968; see *Improvement Era*, November 1968, 60–63.

sprite of a child seemed unimpressed with the devastation and hopeless futility that surrounded her and was scrambling over the rubble to add new leaves to her collection.

She had found the one beautiful element in her world—perhaps it would be more proper to say that *she* was the one beautiful element in the scene.

I have not forgotten that little girl. Somehow, to think of her increases my faith. Embodied in the child was the answer to futility; in her there was hope.

Children have a frankness and honesty that is disarming. They possess a simple, implicit faith that is shared by few adults. The Lord instructed His disciples by calling "a little child unto him, and set him in the midst of them, and said, Verily I say unto you, Except ye be converted, and become as little children, ye shall not enter into the kingdom of heaven" (Matthew 18:2–3).

In children there is little pride and little vanity. They eagerly and trustingly respond.

It is little wonder that the Lord chose a mere boy to act as His spokesman in restoring the kingdom of God to the earth. Some have been incredulous over the fact—and it is a fact—that God the Father and His Son Jesus Christ did reveal themselves to Joseph Smith when he was but in his fifteenth year.

More remarkable perhaps than the vision itself was the naive, implicit faith with which the boy had sought answer to his prayers in a secluded grove.

Faith and humility go hand in hand. The person who can acknowledge his dependence upon God and accept a child-parent relationship with Him has prepared a growing place for faith.

The Book of Mormon gives an account of a man who had tremendous faith. The brother of Jared went up on the mountain with sixteen small stones. He had in mind having the Lord touch them that there might be light in the Jaredite vessels as they traveled. His petition was granted, and as the Lord touched the stones, the brother of Jared saw the finger of the Lord. He fell down before Him, saying that he knew not that the Lord had flesh and blood. The Lord said unto him:

"Because of thy faith thou hast seen that I shall take upon me flesh and blood; and never has man come before me with such exceeding faith as thou hast; for were it not so ye could not have seen my finger. Sawest thou more than this?"

The answer was monumentally courageous: "Nay; Lord, show thyself unto me" (Ether 3:9–10).

In the Lord's answer, the choice of a simple word, the word *shall,* is a marvelous commentary on faith. Now there was a test of faith involved, as the Lord asked, "Believest thou the words which I *shall* speak?" (Ether 3:11; italics added). Interesting, isn't it, that the brother of Jared was not asked, "Believest thou the words which I *have* spoken?" It didn't relate to the past. It related to the future. The brother of Jared was asked to commit himself on something that had not yet happened. He was to confirm his belief in that which the Lord had not yet spoken.

There are few individuals, indeed, who would command such faith from any of us. To few people would we commit ourselves to believe that which they were going to say. It takes faith to be willing to commit oneself that way.

The Lord said, by way of testing the brother of Jared, "Believest thou the words which I *shall* speak?" The brother of Jared confirmed his great faith by answering, "Yea, Lord, I know that thou speakest the truth, for thou art a God of truth, and canst not lie" (Ether 3:12). When the Lord saw that he would believe anything that He said, the Lord showed Himself to him. The brother of Jared had actually seen; now he had knowledge. The record confirms:

"And because of the knowledge of this man he could not be kept from beholding within the veil; and he saw the finger of Jesus, which, when he saw, he fell with fear; for he knew that it was the finger of the Lord; and he had faith no longer, for he knew, nothing doubting" (Ether 3:19).

Faith, to be faith, must center on something that is not known. Faith, to be faith, must go beyond that for which there is confirming evidence. Faith, to be faith, must go into the unknown. Faith, to be faith, must walk to the edge of the light and then a few steps into the darkness. If everything has to be known, if everything has to be explained, if everything has to be certified, then there is no need for faith. Indeed, there is no room for it.

The prophet Alma said:

"Yea, there are many who do say: If thou wilt show unto us a sign from heaven, then we shall know of a surety; then we shall believe.

"Now I ask, is this faith? Behold, I say unto you, Nay; for if a man knoweth a thing he hath no cause to believe, for he knoweth it. . . .

"And now as I said concerning faith—faith is *not* to have a perfect knowledge of things; therefore if ye have faith ye hope for things which are not seen, which are true" (Alma 32:17–18, 21; italics added).

There are two kinds of faith. One of them functions ordinarily in the life of every soul. It is the kind of faith born by experience; it gives us certainty that a new day will dawn, that spring will come, that growth will take place. It is the kind of faith that relates us with confidence to that which is scheduled to happen. This kind of faith was exemplified by the little Japanese girl.

There is another kind of faith, rare indeed. This is the kind of faith that *causes* things to happen. It is the kind of faith that is worthy and prepared and unyielding, and it calls forth things that otherwise would not be. It is the kind of faith that moves people. It is the kind of faith that sometimes moves things. Few men possess it. It comes by gradual growth. It is a marvelous, even a transcendent power, a power as real and as invisible as electricity. Directed and channeled, it has great effect.

But faith must be faith. A man was "experimenting" with faith. He had spoken of his certainty that an event would transpire. His desires were not brought to pass. The event he so much yearned for did not happen. Afterward, his bitter comment was, "Well, you see, it didn't happen. I didn't think it would."

In a world filled with skepticism and doubt, the expression "seeing is believing" promotes the attitude, "You show me, and I will believe." We want all of the proof and all of the evidence first. It seems hard to take things on faith.

When will we learn that in spiritual things it works the other way around—that believing is seeing? Spiritual belief precedes spiritual knowledge. When we believe in things that are not seen but are nevertheless true, then we have faith.

The Prophet Joseph Smith declared:

"Never be discouraged . . . if I were sunk in the lowest pit of Nova Scotia, with the Rocky Mountains piled on me, I would hang on, exercise faith, and keep up good courage, and I would come out on top" (in John Henry Evans, *Joseph Smith: An American Prophet,* Classics in Mormon Literature edition [1989], 9).

Faith can increase. It will move forward as a light before us. Sometimes the fogs and mists of doubt are so thick and enshroud us so fully that only the most penetrating and persistent faith will send a beam beyond it.

As we exercise faith, we can do as did Nephi, who said: "And I was led by the Spirit, not knowing beforehand the things which I should do" (1 Nephi 4:6).

2

"THE TOUCH OF THE MASTER'S HAND"

It is my purpose to ease the pain of those who suffer from the very unpleasant feeling of guilt. I feel like the doctor who begins his treatment by saying, "Now, this may hurt a little. . . ."

Every one of us has at least tasted the pain of conscience which follows our mistakes.

John said that "if we say that we have no sin, we deceive ourselves, and the truth is not in us" (1 John 1:8). Then he said it more strongly, "If we say that we have not sinned, we make [the Lord] a liar, and his word is not in us" (1 John 1:10).

All of us sometime, and some of us much of the time, suffer remorse of conscience from things we did wrong or things we left undone. That feeling of guilt is to the spirit what pain is to the physical body.

But guilt can be harder to bear than physical pain. Physical pain is nature's warning system that signals something needs to be changed or

From an address given at general conference, March 31, 2001; see *Ensign*, May 2001, 22–24.

cleansed or treated, perhaps even removed by surgery. Guilt, the pain of our conscience, cannot be healed the same way.

If you are burdened with depressing feelings of guilt or disappointment, of failure or shame, there is a cure. My intent is not to hurt your tender feelings but to help you and help those you love.

The prophets teach how painful guilt can be. As you read what they have said, be prepared for *very* strong words. Even so, what follows does not include the strongest things they have said.

The prophet Alma, describing his feelings of guilt, said, "I was *racked* with eternal *torment,* for my soul was *harrowed up* to the greatest degree and *racked* with all my sins" (Alma 36:12; italics added).

The prophets choose very graphic words.

Racked means "tortured" (see Mosiah 27:29; Alma 36:12, 16–17; Mormon 9:3). Anciently a rack was a framework on which the victim was laid with each ankle and wrist tied to a spindle which could then be turned to cause unbearable pain.

A harrow is a frame with spikes through it. When pulled across the ground, it rips and tears into the soil. The scriptures frequently speak of souls and minds being "harrowed up" with guilt (see 2 Nephi 9:47; Alma 14:6; 15:3; 36:12, 17, 19; 39:7).

Torment means "to twist," a means of torture so painful that even the innocent would confess (see Mosiah 2:39; 3:25; 5:5; Moroni 8:21).

The prophets speak of the "gall of bitterness" (see Acts 8:23; Mosiah 27:29; Alma 36:18; 41:11; Mormon 8:31; Moroni 8:14) and often compare the pain of guilt to fire and brimstone. *Brimstone* is another name for sulfur.

King Benjamin said that those who are evil will be "consigned to an awful view of their own guilt and abominations, which doth cause them to shrink from the presence of the Lord into a state of misery and endless torment" (Mosiah 3:25).

The Prophet Joseph Smith said: "A man is his own tormentor and his own condemner. . . . The torment of disappointment in the mind of man [or woman] is as exquisite as a lake burning with fire and brim-stone" *(History of The Church of Jesus Christ of Latter-day Saints,* ed. B. H. Roberts, 2d ed. rev., 7 vols. [1932–51], 6:314).

That lake of fire and brimstone, ever burning but never consumed, is the description in the scriptures for hell (see Revelation 20:10; 21:8; 2 Nephi 9:16, 19, 26; 28:23; Jacob 3:11; 6:10; Mosiah 3:27; Alma 12:17; 14:14; D&C 63:17; 76:36).

Suppose there were no cure, no way to ease spiritual pain or to erase the agony of guilt. Suppose each mistake, each sin, were added to the others with the racking, the harrowing up, the torment going on forever. Too many of us needlessly carry burdens of guilt and shame.

The scriptures teach that there "must needs be . . . opposition in all things." If not, "righteousness could not be brought to pass" (2 Nephi 2:11), neither happiness, nor joy, nor redemption.

The third article of faith teaches, "We believe that through the Atonement of Christ, all mankind may be saved, by obedience to the laws and ordinances of the Gospel." The Atonement offers redemption from spiritual death and from suffering caused by sin.

For some reason we think the Atonement of Christ applies *only* at the end of mortal life to redemption from the Fall, from spiritual death. It is much more than that. It is an ever-present power to call upon in everyday life. When we are racked or harrowed up or tormented by guilt or burdened with grief, He can heal us. While we do not fully understand how the Atonement of Christ was made, we can experience "the peace of God, which passeth all understanding" (Philippians 4:7).

The gospel plan is the "great plan of happiness" (Alma 42:8). It is contrary to the nature of God and contrary to the very nature of man to find happiness in sin. "Wickedness never was happiness" (Alma 41:10; see also v. 11).

We know that some anxiety and depression is caused by physical disorders, but much (perhaps most) of it is not pain of the body but of the spirit. Spiritual pain resulting from guilt can be replaced with peace of mind.

In contrast to the hard words condemning sin, listen to the calming, healing words of *mercy,* which balance the harsher words of *justice.*

Alma said: "My soul hath been redeemed from the gall of bitterness and bonds of iniquity. I was in the darkest abyss; but now I behold the marvelous light of God. My soul was racked with eternal torment; but . . . my soul is pained no more" (Mosiah 27:29).

"I did remember all my sins and iniquities, for which I was tormented with the pains of hell. . . .

"And . . . as I was thus racked with torment, while I was harrowed up by the memory of my many sins, behold, I remembered also to have heard my father prophesy unto the people concerning the coming of one Jesus Christ, a Son of God, to atone for the sins of the world.

"Now, as my mind caught hold upon this thought, I cried within my heart: O Jesus, thou Son of God, have mercy on me, who am in the gall of bitterness, and am encircled about by the everlasting chains of death.

"And now, behold, when I thought this, I could remember my pains no more; yea, I was harrowed up by the memory of my sins no more.

"And oh, what joy, and what marvelous light I did behold; yea, my soul was filled with joy as exceeding as was my pain!" (Alma 36:13–20).

We all make mistakes. Sometimes we harm ourselves and seriously injure others in ways that we alone cannot repair. We break things that we alone cannot fix. It is then in our nature to feel guilt and humiliation and suffering, which we alone cannot cure. That is when the healing power of the Atonement will help.

The Lord said, "Behold, I, God, have suffered these things for all, that they might not suffer if they would repent" (D&C 19:16).

If Christ had not made His Atonement, the penalties for mistakes would be added one on the other. Life would be hopeless. But He willingly sacrificed in order that we might be redeemed. And He said, "Behold, he who has repented of his sins, the same is forgiven, and I, the Lord, remember them no more" (D&C 58:42; see also Hebrews 8:12; 10:17).

Ezekiel said: "If the wicked restore the pledge, give again that he had robbed, walk in the statutes of life, without committing iniquity; he shall surely live, he shall not die.

"None of his sins that he hath committed shall be mentioned unto him" (Ezekiel 33:15–16).

Think of that: our sins shall not even be mentioned!

We can even "retain a remission of [our] sins" (Mosiah 4:12; see also 2 Nephi 25:26; 31:17; Mosiah 3:13; 4:11; 15:11; Alma 4:14; 7:6; 12:34; 13:16; Helaman 14:13; 3 Nephi 12:2; 30:2; Moroni 8:25; 10:33). Baptism by immersion is for the remission of our sins. That covenant can be renewed by partaking of the sacrament each week (see D&C 27:2).

The Atonement has practical, personal, everyday value; apply it in your life. It can be activated with so simple a beginning as prayer. You will not thereafter be free from trouble and mistakes but can erase the guilt through repentance and be at peace.

I quoted the third article of faith. It has two parts: "We believe that through the Atonement of Christ, all mankind may be saved, [then the conditions] by obedience to the laws and ordinances of the Gospel."

Justice requires that there be a punishment (see Alma 42:16–22). Guilt is not erased without pain. There are laws to obey and ordinances to receive, and there are penalties to pay.

Physical pain requires treatment and a change in lifestyle. So it is with spiritual pain. There must be repentance and discipline, most of which is self-discipline. But to restore our innocence after serious transgressions, there must be confession to our bishop, who is the appointed judge.

The Lord promised, "A new heart . . . will I give you, and a new spirit will I put within you" (Ezekiel 36:26). That spiritual heart surgery, like in the body, may cause you pain and require a change in habits and conduct. In both cases, recovery brings renewed life and peace of mind.

When the heavens were opened and the Father and the Son stood before Joseph Smith, the Father spoke seven words: *"This is My Beloved Son. Hear Him!"* (Joseph Smith–History 1:17). Revelation followed revelation, and The Church of Jesus Christ of Latter-day Saints (see D&C 115:4) was organized. He Himself declared it to be "the only true and living church upon the face of the whole earth" (D&C 1:30).

Peter, James, and John restored the higher priesthood, and John the Baptist the Aaronic Priesthood. The fulness of the gospel was revealed.

Consistent with the revelations which came and yet come to His Church, all that has been printed or preached or sung or built or taught or broadcast has been to the end that men and women and children can know the redeeming influence of the Atonement of Christ in their everyday lives and be at peace.

He said, "Peace I leave with you, my peace I give unto you" (John 14:27).

As one who stands among His Apostles, I testify of Him and of the ever-present power of His Atonement.

From the lofty words of *justice* and *mercy* and of *warning* and *hope* in the verses of scripture, I turn to the very same message in verses of a simple poem:

> *'Twas battered and scarred, and the auctioneer*
> *Thought it scarcely worth his while*
> *To waste much time on the old violin,*
> *But held it up with a smile:*
>
> *"What am I bidden, good folks," he cried,*
> *"Who'll start the bidding for me?"*

"A dollar, a dollar"; then, "Two!" "Only two?
Two dollars, and who'll make it three?

Three dollars, once; three dollars, twice;
Going for three—" But no,
From the room, far back, a gray-haired man
Came forward and picked up the bow;

Then, wiping the dust from the old violin,
And tightening the loose strings,
He played a melody pure and sweet
As a caroling angel sings.

The music ceased, and the auctioneer,
With a voice that was quiet and low,
Said, "What am I bid for the old violin?"
And he held it up with the bow.

"A thousand dollars, and who'll make it two?
Two thousand! And who'll make it three?
Three thousand, once, three thousand, twice,
And going, and gone!" said he.

The people cheered, but some of them cried,
"We do not quite understand
What changed its worth." Swift came the reply:
"The touch of a master's hand."

And many a man with life out of tune,
And battered and scarred with sin,
Is auctioned cheap to the thoughtless crowd,
Much like the old violin.

A "mess of pottage," a glass of wine,
A game—and he travels on.
He's "going" once, and "going" twice,
He's "going" and almost "gone."

But the Master comes, and the foolish crowd
Never can quite understand
The worth of a soul and the change that's wrought
By the touch of the Master's hand.

(Myra Brooks Welch, "The Touch of the Master's Hand," in *Best-Loved Poems of the LDS People,* ed. Jack M. Lyon and others [1996], 182–83)

3

"CLOVEN TONGUES OF FIRE"

Travel with me half a world away and two millennia ago to the river Jordan with John the Baptist. He preached, "I . . . baptize you with water unto repentance: but he that cometh after me is mightier than I, . . . he shall baptize you with the Holy Ghost, and with fire" (Matthew 3:11).

"Then [came] Jesus from Galilee to Jordan unto John, to be baptized of him" (Matthew 3:13).

"[When Jesus came] up . . . out of the water: . . . the heavens were opened unto him, and he saw the Spirit of God [the Holy Ghost] descending like a dove, and lighting upon him:

"And lo a voice from heaven, saying, This is my beloved Son, in whom I am well pleased" (Matthew 3:16–17).

Jesus then went into the wilderness; Lucifer came tempting Him (see Matthew 4:1–11). Jesus deflected each temptation with scripture.

"It is written, Man shall not live by bread alone" (Matthew 4:4).

From an address given at general conference, April 1, 2000; see *Ensign*, May 2000, 7–9.

"It is written again, Thou shalt not tempt the Lord thy God" (Matthew 4:7).

"It is written, Thou shalt worship the Lord thy God, and him only shalt thou serve" (Matthew 4:10).

Think on it carefully. When facing Perdition himself, the Lord drew upon scriptures for protection.

Jesus chose from among His disciples twelve whom He ordained Apostles: Peter, James, and John; Andrew, Philip, Bartholomew, Thomas, Matthew, Simon, James, Jude, and Judas. They were ordinary men described by the Pharisees as "unlearned and ignorant" (Acts 4:13).

The Twelve followed Him. He taught them.

He commanded them to teach all nations, baptizing all who would believe (see Matthew 28:19).

Before He left, He promised, "The Comforter, which is the Holy Ghost, whom the Father will send in my name, he shall teach you all things, and bring all things to your remembrance, whatsoever I have said unto you" (John 14:26).

Jesus was crucified. On the third day He rose from the tomb. He gave further instruction to His Apostles; and then, before He ascended, He said, "Behold, I send the promise of my Father upon you: but tarry ye in the city of Jerusalem, until ye be [endowed] with power from on high" (Luke 24:49).

That power was not long in coming. On the day of Pentecost, the Twelve were assembled in a house:

"Suddenly there came a sound . . . of a rushing mighty wind, . . .

"And there appeared unto them cloven tongues like as of fire, and it sat upon each of them.

"And they were all filled with the Holy Ghost" (Acts 2:2–4).

With that the Twelve were fully empowered. When they spoke that day, the people marveled, for each heard it in their own language— eighteen different languages (see Acts 2:7–11).

The Apostles set out to baptize all who would believe on their words. But baptism unto repentance was not enough (see Acts 2:38). Paul found twelve men who had already been baptized by John the Baptist and asked, "Have ye received the Holy Ghost . . . ? [They replied], We have not so much as heard whether there be any Holy Ghost" (Acts 19:2; see also *Teachings of the Prophet Joseph Smith,* sel. Joseph Fielding Smith [1976], 263, 336).

"They were [then] baptized in the name of the Lord Jesus" (Acts 19:5), and "Paul . . . laid his hands upon them, [and] the Holy Ghost came on them" (Acts 19:6).

The pattern was set, as it had been from the beginning (see Moses 6:65–66). Entrance into the Church of Jesus Christ is through "baptism by immersion for the remission of sins" (Articles of Faith 1:4). Then, in a separate ordinance, the priceless gift of the Holy Ghost is conferred "by the laying on of hands by those who are in authority, to preach the Gospel and administer in the ordinances" (Articles of Faith 1:5).

Despite opposition, the Twelve established the Church of Jesus Christ; and despite persecution, it flourished. But as the centuries passed, the flame flickered and dimmed. Ordinances were changed or abandoned. The line was broken, and the authority to confer the Holy Ghost as a gift was gone. The Dark Ages of apostasy settled over the world.

But always, as it had from the beginning, the Spirit of God inspired worthy souls (see 1 Nephi 10:17–19).

We owe an immense debt to the protestors and the reformers who preserved the scriptures and translated them. They knew something had been lost. They kept the flame alive as best they could. Many of them were martyrs. But protesting was not enough; nor could reformers restore that which was gone.

In time, a great diversity of churches arose. And then, when all was prepared, the Father and the Son appeared to the boy Joseph in the Grove, and those words spoken at the river Jordan were heard once again: *"This is My Beloved Son. Hear Him!"* (Joseph Smith–History 1:17).

Joseph Smith became the instrument of the Restoration.

John the Baptist restored "the Priesthood of Aaron, which holds the keys of the ministering of angels, and of the gospel of repentance, and of baptism by immersion for the remission of sins" (D&C 13).

Peter, James, and John restored the office of Apostle with the higher priesthood. With it came authority to confer the supernally precious gift of the Holy Ghost (see D&C 27:12–13).

On 6 April 1830, The Church of Jesus Christ of Latter-day Saints was organized. The Brethren set about to teach and to baptize. Nine months later came a correction, a revelation:

"Thou didst baptize by water unto repentance, but they received not the Holy Ghost;

"But now I give unto thee a commandment, that thou shalt baptize by water, and they shall receive the Holy Ghost by the laying on of the hands, even as the apostles of old" (D&C 35:5–6).

One month later, that commandment was repeated: "On as many as ye shall baptize with water, ye shall lay your hands, and they shall receive the gift of the Holy Ghost" (D&C 39:23).

The gift is to all who repent and are baptized—boys and girls alike, women and men the same.

We live in troubled times—very troubled times. We hope, we pray, for better days. But that is not to be. The prophecies tell us that. We will not as a people, as families, or as individuals be exempt from the trials to come. No one will be spared the trials common to home and family, work, disappointment, grief, health, aging, ultimately death.

What then shall we do? That question was asked of the Twelve on the day of Pentecost. Peter answered, "Repent, and be baptized everyone of you in the name of Jesus Christ for the remission of sins, and ye shall receive the gift of the Holy Ghost" (Acts 2:38).

He told them, "The promise is unto you, and to your children, and to all that are afar off" (Acts 2:39).

That same question—"What shall we do?" (Acts 2:37)—was asked of the prophet Nephi. He gave the same answer that Peter would give: "Take upon you the name of Christ, by baptism . . . , then cometh the baptism of fire and of the Holy Ghost" (2 Nephi 31:13).

"Do ye not remember that I said unto you that after ye had received the Holy Ghost ye could speak with the tongue of angels? . . .

"Angels speak by the power of the Holy Ghost; wherefore, they speak the words of Christ. Wherefore, I said unto you, feast upon the words of Christ; for behold, the words of Christ will tell you all things what ye should do.

"Wherefore, now after I have spoken these words, if ye cannot understand them it will be because ye ask not, neither do ye knock; wherefore, ye are not brought into the light, but must perish in the dark.

"For behold, again I say unto you that if ye will enter in by the way, and receive the Holy Ghost, it will show unto you all things what ye should do" (2 Nephi 32:2–5).

We need not live in fear of the future. We have every reason to rejoice and little reason to fear. If we follow the promptings of the Spirit, we will be safe, whatever the future holds. We will be shown what to do.

Christ promised that "the Father [would send] another Comforter, . . .

"Even the Spirit of truth; whom the world cannot receive, because it seeth him not, neither knoweth him: but ye know him; for he dwelleth with you, and shall be in you" (John 14:16–17).

Too many of us are like those whom the Lord said "[came] with a broken heart and a contrite spirit, . . . [and] at the time of their conversion, were baptized with fire and with the Holy Ghost, *and they knew it not*" (3 Nephi 9:20; italics added).

Imagine that: "And they knew it not." It is not unusual for one to have received the gift and not really know it.

I fear this supernal gift is being obscured by programs and activities and schedules and so many meetings. There are so many places to go, so many things to do in this noisy world. We can be too busy to pay attention to the promptings of the Spirit.

The voice of the Spirit is a still, small voice—a voice that is felt rather than heard. It is a spiritual voice that comes into the mind as a thought put into your heart.

All over the world, ordinary men, women, and children, not completely aware that they have the gift, bless their families, teach, preach, and minister by the Spirit within them.

In every language, the Spirit of God—the Holy Ghost—guides, or can guide, every member of the Church. Everyone is invited to come and repent and be baptized and receive of this sacred gift.

Despite opposition, the Church will flourish; and despite persecution, it will grow.

Joseph Smith was asked, "How does your religion differ from other religions?" He replied, "All other considerations were contained in the gift of the Holy Ghost" (see *History of The Church of Jesus Christ of Latter-day Saints,* ed. B. H. Roberts, 2d ed. rev., 7 vols. [1932–51], 4:42).

This gift is awakened with prayer and cultivated "by obedience to the laws and ordinances of the Gospel" (Articles of Faith 1:3).

It can be smothered through transgression and neglect.

And soon we learn that the tempter—the adversary—uses those same channels of the mind and heart to inspire us to evil, to laziness, to contention, even to acts of darkness. He can take over our thoughts and lead us to mischief.

But each of us has agency; ever and always light presides over darkness.

The priesthood is structured to ensure an unbroken line of authority to baptize and confer the Holy Ghost. Always nearby are leaders and teachers called and set apart to teach us and to correct us. We can learn to sort out the promptings from the temptations and follow the inspiration of the Holy Ghost.

It is a glorious time to live! No matter what trials await us, we can find the answer to that question, "What shall we do?" We, and those we love, will be guided and corrected and protected, and we will be comforted.

The Lord said: "Peace I leave with you, my peace I give unto you: not as the world giveth, give I unto you. Let not your heart be troubled, neither let it be afraid" (John 14:27).

As surely as I know that I am here and you are there, I know that Jesus is the Christ. He lives! I know the gift of the Holy Ghost, a sacred spiritual power, can be a constant companion to every soul who will receive it. I pray that the witness of the Holy Ghost will confirm this testimony to you.

4

"THE PEACEABLE FOLLOWERS OF CHRIST"

In his closing sermon, the prophet Moroni recorded the words of his father, Mormon, who said, "I . . . speak unto you that are of the church, that are *the peaceable followers of Christ,*" and he spoke further of our "peaceable walk with the children of men" (Moroni 7:3–4; italics added).

My preparation for this discussion has been challenging. I have determined to do something I have seldom done before—to present a message intended for someone who is not likely to read it.

My message is for those who teach and write and produce films which claim that The Church of Jesus Christ of Latter-day Saints is not a Christian church and that we, the members, are not Christians.

When faced with that assertion, I find myself disadvantaged— cornered, challenged. I find it difficult to respond without saying that such individuals are uninformed and unfair and not consistent with the spirit of Christian brotherhood. But confrontation is not the way

From an address given at a Church Educational System fireside, Brigham Young University, February 1, 1998; see *Ensign*, April 1998, 62–67.

to reason through a challenge such as this. The much better approach is to teach, to remain "peaceable followers of Christ."

If they claimed that we do not fit the Christian mold they have designed for themselves or that we do not conform to *their* definition of Christian, it would be easier to reason together. But we need not justify what we believe, only to teach and to explain. Others can accept or reject as they please. They have their agency.

There is more to it than simply writing a definition of what a Christian is and then rejecting anyone who does not conform to it. If we really are not Christians, there are some things that are left for them to explain.

For example, suppose someone who had never heard of The Church of Jesus Christ of Latter-day Saints came upon one of our hymnbooks and asked himself, "Who published this? What do they believe? What kind of people are they?"

He would find it filled with hymns and anthems which testify of Christ, many of which are revered by Christians throughout the world: "Jesus, Lover of My Soul," "Jesus, the Very Thought of Thee," "The Lord Is My Shepherd," and more than thirty others.

He would find more than a hundred hymns written by Latter-day Saints which teach of Christ. In the spirit of worship, these hymns teach of the ministry of our Lord, our Redeemer. We sing reverently of His Crucifixion, His sacrifice for our sins, His Resurrection, His Atonement, His Ascension.

These hymns certainly are not the voice of non-Christians. Instead they reveal a people of devotion and faith who love, indeed worship, our Savior and Redeemer. Consider these verses selected from a few of them.

The first one, "Jesus, Once of Humble Birth," was written by Elder Parley P. Pratt, who was a member of the Quorum of the Twelve Apostles:

Jesus, once of humble birth,
Now in glory comes to earth.
Once he suffered grief and pain;
Now he comes on earth to reign. . . .

Once a meek and lowly Lamb,
Now the Lord, the great I Am.
Once upon the cross he bowed;
Now his chariot is the cloud. . . .

Once he groaned in blood and tears;
Now in glory he appears.
Once rejected by his own,
Now their King he shall be known.

(*Hymns*, no. 196)

The next verses, from "Behold the Great Redeemer Die," were written by Eliza R. Snow, an early president of the Relief Society:

Behold the great Redeemer die,
A broken law to satisfy.
He dies a sacrifice for sin, . . .
That man may live and glory win. . . .

He died, and at the awful sight
The sun in shame withdrew its light!
Earth trembled, and all nature sighed
In dread response, "A God has died!"

He lives—he lives. We humbly now
Around these sacred symbols bow,
And seek, as Saints of latter days,
To do his will and live his praise.

(*Hymns*, no. 191)

Finally, consider these verses from "How Great the Wisdom and the Love," also written by Eliza R. Snow:

> *How great the wisdom and the love*
> *That filled the courts on high*
> *And sent the Savior from above*
> *To suffer, bleed, and die!*
>
> *His precious blood he freely spilt;*
> *His life he freely gave,*
> *A sinless sacrifice for guilt,*
> *A dying world to save.*
>
> *By strict obedience Jesus won*
> *The prize with glory rife:*
> *"Thy will, O God, not mine be done,"*
> *Adorned his mortal life.*
>
> *He marked the path and led the way,*
> *And ev'ry point defines*
> *To light and life and endless day*
> *Where God's full presence shines.*
>
> (*Hymns*, no. 195)

Is that the voice of non-Christians?

More than fifty hymns of transcendent beauty and devotion speak in pure testimony of the Lord. They invite a spirit of reverence and worship of the Lord into the meetings of the Latter-day Saints.

How could words like that be written by non-Christians? Was it not the Master who asked, "Do men gather grapes of thorns, or figs of thistles?" (Matthew 7:16). How do those who say we are not Christians account for such reverent tributes to the Lord?

One reason for my feeling challenged by this claim that we are not Christians is that I do not know how to answer it without quoting from revelations from scriptures which they reject.

Unless these critics at least understand why we accept such revelations, we will never come to agree.

Consider the name: The Church of Jesus Christ of Latter-day Saints.

On this subject, the Lord Himself has spoken more than once. Listen to this account from the Book of Mormon:

"And it came to pass that as the disciples of Jesus were journeying and were preaching the things which they had both heard and seen, and were baptizing in the name of Jesus, it came to pass that the disciples were gathered together and were united in mighty prayer and fasting.

"And Jesus again showed himself unto them, for they were praying unto the Father in his name; and Jesus came and stood in the midst of them, and said unto them: What will ye that I shall give unto you?

"And they said unto him: Lord, we will that thou wouldst tell us the name whereby we shall call this church; for there are disputations among the people concerning this matter.

"And the Lord said unto them: Verily, verily, I say unto you, why is it that the people should murmur and dispute because of this thing?

"Have they not read the scriptures, which say ye must take upon you the name of Christ, which is my name? For by this name shall ye be called at the last day;

"And whoso taketh upon him my name, and endureth to the end, the same shall be saved at the last day.

"Therefore, *whatsoever ye shall do, ye shall do it in my name;* therefore ye shall call the church in my name; and ye shall call upon the Father in my name that he will bless the church for my sake.

"And how be it my church save it be called in my name? For if a church be called in Moses' name then it be Moses' church; or if it be called in the name of a man then it be the church of a man; but if it be called in my name then it is my church, if it so be that they are built upon my gospel.

"Verily I say unto you, that ye are built upon my gospel; therefore *ye shall call whatsoever things ye do call, in my name;* therefore if ye call upon the Father, for the church, if it be in my name the Father will hear you" (3 Nephi 27:1–9; italics added).

In a revelation given in 1838, the Lord spoke to "the elders and people of my Church of Jesus Christ of Latter-day Saints, scattered abroad in all the world," saying, "For thus shall my church be called in the last days, even The Church of Jesus Christ of Latter-day Saints" (D&C 115:3–4).

Others refer to us as Mormons. I do not mind if they use that title. However, sometimes we are prone ourselves to say "Mormon Church." I do not think it best for us to do so.

The First Presidency has told us to "keep in mind that this is the Church of Jesus Christ; please emphasize that fact in making contacts with others. . . . We feel that some may be misled by the too frequent use of the term 'Mormon Church'" ("News of the Church," *Ensign,* March 1983, 79; see also First Presidency Letter, 23 February 2001).

We obey the commandment "Whatsoever ye shall do, ye shall do it in my name" (3 Nephi 27:7). Every prayer we offer is in His name. Every ordinance performed is in His name. Every baptism, confirmation, blessing, ordination, every sermon, every testimony is concluded with the invocation of His sacred name. It is in His name that we heal the sick and perform other miracles of which we do not, cannot, speak.

In the sacrament we take upon ourselves the name of Christ. We covenant to remember Him and keep His commandments. He is present in all that we believe.

Several years ago Sister Packer and I went to Oxford University. We were looking for the records of my seventh great-grandfather John Packer. Dr. Poppelwell, the head of Christ's College at Oxford, was kind enough to have the archivist of Christ's College bring the records. There in the entries for the year 1583, we found my ancestor's name: John Packer.

The following year we returned to Oxford to present a beautifully bound set of the standard works to the library at Christ's College. It seemed a bit awkward for the head of Christ's College, Dr. Poppelwell. Perhaps he thought we were not really Christians. So he called for the college chaplain to receive the books.

Before handing them to the chaplain, I opened the Topical Guide and showed him references to one subject: eighteen pages, very fine print, single-spaced, listing references to the one subject of Jesus Christ. It is the most comprehensive compilation of scriptural references on the subject of Jesus Christ that has ever been assembled in the history of the world—a testimony from the Old and New Testaments, Book of Mormon, Doctrine and Covenants, and Pearl of Great Price.

However you follow these references, I told him, side to side, up and down, book to book, subject after subject, you will find that they are a consistent, harmonious witness to the divinity of the mission of the Lord Jesus Christ—His birth, His life, His teachings, His Crucifixion, His Resurrection, and His Atonement.

The atmosphere changed and we were cordially given a tour, including an excavation revealing recently discovered murals which dated to Roman days.

Among those references listed in the Topical Guide is the one from the Book of Mormon: Another Testament of Jesus Christ:

"We preach of Christ, we prophesy of Christ, and we write according to our prophecies, that our children may know to what source they may look for a remission of their sins" (2 Nephi 25:26).

Christ dominates that testament page by page. He is referred to in 3,925 verses, more than half of the 6,607 verses in the book. Beginning with the title page, where the purpose of the book is given as "the convincing of the Jew and Gentile that Jesus is the Christ, the Eternal God," He is referred to as the Son of God, the Redeemer of the world, the Only Begotten of the Father, and nearly a hundred other titles. In the last phrase of the last sentence of the last verse, verse 6,607, the Savior is referred to as "the great Jehovah, the Eternal Judge" (Moroni

10:34; see also Susan Ward Easton, "Names of Christ in the Book of Mormon," *Ensign,* July 1978, 60–61).

It is one thing to say that we are not their kind of Christian. It is another entirely to characterize us as not being Christian at all.

There are doctrinal beliefs that will continue to be misunderstood and disturb our critics. A few of them are these:

- The statement in the revelation that The Church of Jesus Christ of Latter-day Saints is "the only true and living church upon the face of the whole earth" (D&C 1:30).
- Scriptures in addition to the Bible—the Book of Mormon, Doctrine and Covenants, and Pearl of Great Price.
- Continuing revelation through apostles and prophets.
- The doctrine of the Godhead. The Father, Son, and Holy Ghost are three separate and distinct personages, and "the Father has a body of flesh and bones as tangible as man's" (D&C 130:22).
- We are the literal spirit children of God and thus have the possibility to eventually become as He is.
- Marriages may continue after this life, and families can be forever.
- And, of course, we are not saved by grace alone but saved "after all we can do" (2 Nephi 25:23).

One need not have answers to all those questions to receive the witness of the Spirit, join the Church, and remain faithful therein. There is a knowledge that transcends rational explanations, sacred knowledge that leads to conversion.

While we can provide answers, they will not be satisfactory, however, to those who do not accept continuing revelation. To argue or debate over sacred things usually generates much more heat than light.

There is what I call the principle of prerequisites. That principle operates in school. Without the basic prerequisite course in chemistry, we will have a hard time understanding advanced chemistry, if we ever do. Not that we are not intelligent enough to understand, but a proper foundation simply has not been laid.

Paul told the Corinthians that very thing: "For what man knoweth the things of a man, save the spirit of man which is in him? even so the things of God knoweth no man, but the Spirit of God.

"Now we have received, not the spirit of the world, but the spirit which is of God; that we might know the things that are freely given to us of God.

"Which things also we speak, not in the words which man's wisdom teacheth, but which the Holy Ghost teacheth; comparing spiritual things with spiritual.

"But the natural man receiveth not the things of the Spirit of God: for they are foolishness unto him: neither can he know them, because they are spiritually discerned" (1 Corinthians 2:11–14).

I suppose others are puzzled as to how we attract so many converts, or why members stay in the Church with so many questions we are not able to answer to everyone's satisfaction.

Our critics' belief, based on the Bible, holds that man is saved by grace alone. Theirs is by far the easier way.

Our position, also based on the Bible but strengthened by other scriptures, holds that we are saved by grace "after all we can do" (2 Nephi 25:23), and we are responsible by conduct and by covenants to live the standards of the gospel.

We agree with the Apostle James that "faith, if it hath not works, is dead, being alone," and we say to all those who make such an accusation, "Shew me thy faith without thy works, and I will shew thee my faith by my works" (James 2:17–18).

Buttressed by covenants and ordinances, Latter-day Saints observe the law of the fast, pay tithes and offerings, and send their children on missions, "for we labor diligently to write, to persuade our children, and also our brethren, *to believe in Christ,* and to be reconciled to God;

for we know that it is by grace that we are saved, after all we can do" (2 Nephi 25:23; italics added).

As converts mature spiritually, they gain "a reason [for] the hope that is in [them]" (1 Peter 3:15). The gospel becomes as satisfying to the mind as it is soothing to the heart. We spend our lives learning the things of God. Those difficult questions one by one become testimonies.

"We claim the [right to worship] Almighty God according to the dictates of our own conscience, and allow all men the same privilege, let them worship how, where, or what they may" (Articles of Faith 1:11).

A caution to those who willfully misrepresent us: They may do well to consider what Gamaliel said to his fellow Pharisees after they had arrested the Apostles:

"Then stood there up one in the council, a Pharisee, named Gamaliel, a doctor of the law, had in reputation among all the people, and commanded to put the apostles forth a little space;

"And said unto them, Ye men of Israel, take heed to yourselves what ye intend to do as touching these men.

"For before these days rose up Theudas, boasting himself to be somebody; to whom a number of men, about four hundred, joined themselves: who was slain; and all, as many as obeyed him, were scattered, and brought to nought.

"After this man rose up Judas of Galilee in the days of the taxing, and drew away much people after him: he also perished; and all, even as many as obeyed him, were dispersed.

"And now I say unto you, Refrain from these men, and let them alone: for if this counsel or this work be of men, it will come to nought:

"But if it be of God, ye cannot overthrow it; lest haply ye be found even to fight against God.

"And to him they agreed: and when they had called the apostles, and beaten them, they commanded that they should not speak in the name of Jesus, and let them go" (Acts 5:34–40).

Gamaliel unknowingly agreed with the Lord, who had said, "Every plant, which my heavenly Father hath not planted, shall be rooted up" (Matthew 15:13).

I will tell you we do not talk of downsizing anything in the Church.

And so, the problem is theirs, not ours. We know whom we worship and what we worship and in whose name. They may say we believe because we were brought up that way from our youth. While true of many of us, it is not true of most. Two-thirds of us are converts who come by the waters of baptism by immersion for the remission of sins and the laying on of hands for the gift of the Holy Ghost.

Each one in the Church, born or by convert, must acquire an individual testimony.

While we must act peaceably, we need not submit to unfair accusations and unjustified opposition.

"The Lord had said unto [the Nephites], and also unto their fathers, that: Inasmuch as ye are not guilty of the first offense, neither the second, ye shall not suffer yourselves to be slain by the hands of your enemies" (Alma 43:46).

If our detractors organize to come against us—to disrupt our work (and that has happened before)—there will be those among them who will say, "We ought not to be doing this. This does not feel good. What we are doing is not right." And as surely as we remain "peaceable followers of Christ," a division will rise up among them, and they will ultimately disarm and weaken themselves.

They might learn from an old Spanish saying, "Les salió el tiro por la culata," which translated means, "The bullet came out the wrong end of the gun."

While we take the gospel of Christ to all people, we do not oppose other churches. If you meet someone who challenges our right to the title Christian, do not confront them. Teach them peaceably. We have but to remain humble and peaceable followers of Christ, for He has promised, "I will fight your battles" (D&C 105:14).

The marvelous thing is that the Lord can manage the Church without a professional clergy. In an early revelation, He commanded "that every man might speak in the name of God the Lord, even the Savior of the world;

"That faith also might increase in the earth;

"That mine everlasting covenant might be established;

"That the fulness of my gospel might be proclaimed by the weak and the simple unto the ends of the world" (D&C 1:20–23).

Some of us puzzle over why, of all things, we are said to be un-Christian. But that is our lot. The prophets have told us that opposition goes with the territory. It was ever thus.

Ours is not an easy church to belong to. The gospel requires dedication and sacrifice. It is not an easy church to administer. With the patterns of the priesthood as they are, men and women are called from every walk of life to teach and to lead and to serve. We have members with every level of gospel knowledge, leadership ability, talents, and testimony. We learn to be patient with one another.

Eliza R. Snow wrote "Think Not, When You Gather to Zion":

> *Think not when you gather to Zion,*
> *Your troubles and trials are through,*
> *That nothing but comfort and pleasure*
> *Are waiting in Zion for you:*
> *No, no, 'tis designed as a furnace,*
> *All substance, all textures to try,*
> *To burn all the "wood, hay, and stubble,"*
> *The gold from the dross purify.*
>
> *Think not when you gather to Zion,*
> *That all will be holy and pure;*
> *That fraud and deception are banished,*
> *And confidence wholly secure:*
> *No, no, for the Lord our Redeemer*

Has said that the tares with the wheat
Must grow till the great day of burning
Shall render the harvest complete.

Think not when you gather to Zion,
The Saints here have nothing to do
But to look to your personal welfare,
And always be comforting you.
No; those who are faithful are doing
What they find to do with their might;
To gather the scattered of Israel
They labor by day and by night.

Think not when you gather to Zion,
The prize and the victory won.
Think not that the warfare is ended,
The work of salvation is done.
No, no; for the great prince of darkness
A tenfold exertion will make,
When he sees you go to the fountain,
Where freely the truth you may take.

(*Hymns* [1948], no. 21)

So, with the encouragement of the Spirit, we do the best we can and go peaceably on.

Some years ago I was invited to speak to a group of faculty and students at Harvard University. I, of course, hoped that the gospel message would be accepted and that our meeting would end in a harmony of views. As I prayed that this might result, there came to me a strong impression that this petition would not be granted.

I determined that, however preposterous the talk about angels and golden plates and restoration might be to my audience, I would teach the truth with quiet confidence, for I have a testimony of the truth. If some must come from the meeting unsettled and disturbed, it would not be *me*. Let *them* be disturbed, if they would.

It was as the Spirit foretold. Some in the group shook their heads in amazement that anyone could believe such things. But I was at peace. I had taught the truth, and they could accept it or reject it as they pleased.

There is always the hope, and often it is true, that in any group one person with an open mind and heart may admit one simple thought: "Could it possibly be true?" Combine that thought with sincere prayer, and one more soul enters a private sacred grove to find the answer to the question "Which of all the churches is true, and which should I join?"

As I grow older in age and experience, I grow ever *less* concerned over whether others agree with us. I grow ever *more* concerned that they understand us. If they do understand, they have their agency and can accept or reject the gospel as they please.

It is not an easy thing for us to defend the position that bothers so many others. But, brethren and sisters, never be ashamed of the gospel of Jesus Christ. Never apologize for the sacred doctrines of the gospel. Never feel inadequate and unsettled because you cannot explain them to the satisfaction of all who might inquire of you. Do not be ill at ease or uncomfortable because you can give little more than your conviction.

Be assured that, if you will explain what you know and testify of what you feel, you may plant a seed that will grow and blossom into a testimony of the gospel of Jesus Christ.

"Behold I say unto you, that as these things are true, and as the Lord God liveth, there is none other name given under heaven save it be this Jesus Christ, of which I have spoken, whereby man can be saved" (2 Nephi 25:20).

As one of the Twelve, I bear witness of the Lord Jesus Christ. He lives. He is our Redeemer and our Savior. He presides over this Church. He is no stranger to His servants here, and as we move into the future with quiet confidence, His Spirit will be with us.

PART TWO

PRINCIPLES FOR PERFECTION

5

THE VOICE THAT CAN BE
FELT RATHER THAN HEARD

The subject is the same subject I have always used in speaking to mission president seminars. I usually select a title for talks about the time they are being printed, but this one I got ahead of time. The title is "The Voice That Can Be Felt Rather Than Heard."

There are 128 of you going out to missions all over the world with all of the languages, and you will be presiding over 19,216 missionaries. That is one-third of the missionary force in the Church. You will have great influence, more really than you know. You go with our blessings and our appreciation and our congratulations.

The message is from the Book of Mormon, of course. You might want to read the Book of Mormon again and again and again, and maybe one or two of the things I say will make it a new book because there is a thread that goes through all of the scriptures, but particularly the Book of Mormon, about the still, small voice.

It was recorded in the Old Testament when Elijah went up into

From an address given at a mission presidents' seminar, Provo, Utah, June 25, 2011.

the mountain in a cave. He was looking for what you are looking for right now. "A great and strong wind rent the mountains" (1 Kings 19:11), and the voice of the Lord was not in the wind, nor was it in the earthquake or the fire. Then there was a hush, and "a still small voice" (1 Kings 19:12) spoke to him. We know what that is. We know we can interpret that.

The Prophet Joseph Smith, during the terrible persecutions in Missouri, went to Washington, D.C., to see the president of the United States, really to beg for some help and some protection. The president of the United States, President Martin Van Buren, asked him the first question, "What is the difference between your church and all of the other churches?"

The Prophet answered in five words: "We have the Holy Ghost." And that is the difference (see *History of The Church of Jesus Christ of Latter-day Saints,* ed. B. H. Roberts, 2d ed. rev., 7 vols. [1932–51], 4:42).

He added at one time or another some interesting statements. One of them was "You might as well baptize a bag of sand as a man, if not done in view of the remission of sins and getting of the Holy Ghost. Baptism by water is but half a baptism, and is good for nothing without the other half—that is, the baptism of the Holy Ghost" (*Teachings of the Prophet Joseph Smith,* sel. Joseph Fielding Smith [1976], 314).

In the New Testament there is an incident where Paul was traveling in Ephesus. He met some recent converts and asked them about baptism. They had been baptized unto the baptism of John, which was valid as far as it went.

"[Paul] said unto them, Have ye received the Holy Ghost since ye believed? And they said unto him, We have not so much as heard whether there be any Holy Ghost" (Acts 19:2). Then Paul started over with those men and baptized them again and conferred upon them the gift of the Holy Ghost, which is the power and the voice that we follow.

When Elijah heard the voice, he described it as not a loud voice but a sweet voice, "a still small voice" (1 Kings 19:12), one that we can hear with our inner ear. That is individually given to everyone. Baptism takes place, and then in a separate ordinance the confirmation to The Church of Jesus Christ of Latter-day Saints takes place with holders of the Melchizedek Priesthood laying their hands—it is by the "laying on of hands" (Articles of Faith 1:4) that this is transferred—and conferring upon each member the Holy Ghost.

You have been given the keys of presidency for your mission, a remarkable gift. You have the keys to all things necessary to see you succeed in the work that you are called to do.

In the Book of Mormon, Laman and Lemuel had had a little difficulty with their younger brother. Actually, they had sought his life. Later he was scolding them, and he said, "Ye have seen an angel, and he spake unto you; yea, ye have heard his voice from time to time; and he hath spoken unto you in a still small voice, but ye were past *feeling*, that ye could not *feel* his words" (1 Nephi 17:45; italics added).

When I first read the Book of Mormon, I knew of some of the critics that said that the Book of Mormon is full of errors of one kind or another. One of those is pointed out because you *hear* words, you do not *feel* them. But if you know anything at all, you know that the best word that describes what takes place is the word *feeling*. "Ye were past *feeling*, that ye could not *feel* his words."

In the last part of the book of 2 Nephi, some people who had come into the Church asked an interesting question. They said, "What is it we are supposed to do now we're in the Church?"

Nephi answered: "I suppose that ye ponder somewhat in your hearts concerning that which ye should do after ye have entered in by the way. But, behold, why do ye ponder these things in your hearts?

"Do ye not remember that I said unto you that after ye had received the Holy Ghost ye could speak with the tongue of angels? And now, how could ye speak with the tongue of angels save it were by the Holy Ghost?

"Angels speak by the power of the Holy Ghost; wherefore, they speak the words of Christ. Wherefore, I said unto you, feast upon the words of Christ; for behold, the words of Christ will tell you all things what ye should do" (2 Nephi 32:1–3).

You do not have to know a lot of things that the world places value on to be a successful mission president and the wife of a successful mission president. But there is one essential that you should know, and that is that *feeling*.

I remember being told by President Joseph Fielding Smith about a time when there was a vacancy in the First Presidency, and general conference came and went. There was great anticipation wondering who would be the new Counselor to the First Presidency, but it did not happen. I was standing in one of the board rooms later when President Smith explained that President Heber J. Grant had come in through the north door, and then-Elder Smith and Elder Harold B. Lee approached President Grant and had a question. They said, "I see you didn't nominate a new Counselor at conference." I am sure they did see that!

President Grant said, "No, the man that is to be my Counselor is not ready yet." And then he said, "I know that voice when it speaks." Then, pointing at each of the Brethren, he said, "I felt it when I called you, and I felt it when I called you." As he pointed at Elder Lee, he said it was just as though he had been electrocuted, the power that came from that direction of the Spirit that was present.

At the next conference, President J. Reuben Clark Jr., who was United States Ambassador to Mexico, was called as Second Counselor in the First Presidency.

I think it will comfort some of you to know that was about the first calling President Clark had in the Church. He had gone to Washington, D.C., as a young lawyer, and they held church in the home of a member of the Twelve who was in Congress then. He was traveling a lot, and he did not get the upbringing and did not go through the tutorial or the apprenticeship that we expect of someone coming to high position in the Church. He wondered what to do. All at once, he was called as Second Counselor in the First Presidency of the Church. He had never been a bishop; he had never been a stake president. He, by his own statement, had never been anything, except the Lord knew who he was. So he worried about what he was to do and how he was to do it.

Then he told once that in that burden with that concern, he began to meet with the First Presidency, and he found that it was an expectation that he would speak boldly and directly in giving his opinion of things, and so he did. But President Clark said, "When President Grant would say, 'Brethren, I *feel* this is the way we should go,' when I heard that word *feel,* I stopped counseling because I knew the Lord had spoken." He proved to be a great servant.

You baptize new members in your missions and wonder about them. I remember the missionaries came and said there was a baptism taking place in the font that was in the chapel where the office was located. I went there, and they introduced me to a woman. I thought, "Well, the missionaries will get anybody that they can persuade for baptism." I thought she was in no way ready by way of experience. She did not have the spiritual upbringing nor had she had an apprenticeship, and here the missionaries—these foolish young missionaries that do not know much of anything except they know everything—had brought her to be baptized.

About a month later I went to church in the Cambridge Ward. As I was coming out of church this woman came up the walk. She looked slightly familiar to me. Then I recognized this was the woman that the elders had brought in from anywhere or everywhere and baptized. I could not believe the transformation that had taken place with her. She had conferred upon her this gift of the Holy Ghost.

That is about all you need to know, how to *feel* that voice. We know from the scriptures that it is a voice of warning. It is a voice of teaching.

You will find that you will not make any mistakes that you are not warned about first. The gospel is kind of trial and error. You may wonder why you did something and think, "Well, that's a blunder. I hope the Brethren don't hear about it!" You will later find out that it was not a mistake. You will not make any mistake. You would have to overrule the Spirit to do that. If the Spirit is right, then you go ahead.

Read again the Book of Mormon, because that book particularly is full of direct references, key words—hidden words, as it were—on this matter of the voice that is *felt* rather than being *heard.* That feeling can come any time. It can come in crowded places. It is helpful sometimes to seek the quiet and prayerfully prepare yourself for the direction you want. But it will come to you. It will come when you need it.

If you can take each elder and sister and teach them that, then their mission will not be measured by the number of baptisms they had but by what has happened to them. Sometimes the mission is for the missionary to shape him up for future activities of life.

I remember one young man came to me and said, "I've been nearly a year in the mission field. I haven't succeeded. What's wrong with me? What am I doing wrong?"

Getting a sense and feeling of him, I realized he was not doing anything wrong. He just had not been doing the right things long enough. And he sits here now having been set apart as mission president. He needed to come of age in the mission field.

There are about a dozen key scriptures, most of them, interestingly enough, in the Book of Mormon. The Bible and Doctrine and Covenants, of course, and the Pearl of Great Price also hold instruction against the power that you will need.

But we are not worried about you. First, we do not have time!

Someone talked to President Spencer W. Kimball once. Actually, one of his old friends chastised him. He had bought a new car. It was a Cadillac. He bought it because in those days we traveled mostly by car, and he could afford it. His friend said to him, "Spencer, you're on the wrong track! You'll be prideful driving a car like that."

When President Kimball told me this, he said, "That night I thought almost all night, then wondered, 'When would I have an extra second to become prideful? It can't squeeze itself in.'"

President Kimball was president of a stake in Arizona, and he was a banker. One day he left the bank, walked down the street to a store, and went in to a man that was there and said, "Jack, we want you to be president of the Young Men in the stake."

He said, "Ah, Spencer, I couldn't do anything like that."

Well, President Kimball tried to persuade him and coax him with no success. He went back to the bank and sat all day smoldering with his failure. Then it dawned on him what he had not done. He left the bank, went down the street, and met the man again in his store. This time he said, "I want to start over. Last Sunday the stake presidency met to consider a vacancy in the Young Men's president. We prayed as to who the Lord wanted, and we became united. As a servant of the Lord, I come to call you to that position."

This reluctant man said, "Well, Spencer, if you are going to put it that way!"

He said, "I put it that way!"

It is a marvelous thing to have the Church, with all of the leadership of the Church. You may think that we who are up in the seats on the stand in conference think more of ourselves than we do. We have that kind of struggle of trying to be good enough. But the one thing we have learned is that the Lord can work even with us. It is who we are and what we are.

We open new nations and wonder, "Well, where will they get leadership in that nation? There is nobody there that is a member of the Church." But we just say, "Not yet, but we'll create what we need." And the elders will go out and begin baptizing, and they will begin coming to church. In due time, it is necessary to organize a stake there. One of us will go there and ask the Lord who He wants to be president of the stake, and He will tell us. We will go on our way and not return for months. Then they are on their own, except that they are never on their own.

In 3 Nephi, it tells of an incident where they prayed to the Lord, and He appeared to them. That has always amazed me because it was just as though it was automatic. They prayed to him, and there He was. It is not quite that easy, but if necessary, it can be that easy.

He said, "What will ye that I shall give unto you?

"And they said unto him: Lord, we will that thou wouldst tell us the name whereby we shall call this church; for there are disputations among the people concerning this matter.

"And the Lord"—I think slightly impatient—"said: . . . Why is it that the people should murmur and dispute because of this thing?

"Have they not read the scriptures, which say ye must take upon you the name of Christ?"

Then He explained that they were to name the Church in His name. "For if a church be called in Moses' name then it be Moses' church; or if it be called in the name of a man then it be the church of a man; but if it be called in my name then it is my church, if it so be that they are built upon my gospel.

"Verily I say unto you, that ye are built upon my gospel; therefore ye shall call whatsoever things ye do call, in my name; therefore if ye call upon the Father, for the church, if it be in my name the Father will hear you;

"And if it so be that the church is built upon my gospel then will the Father show forth his own works in it" (3 Nephi 27:2–5, 8–10).

You have been told to "always pray unto the Father in my name" (3 Nephi 18:19)—always in the name of Jesus Christ. There is great power in that.

I would like to give you an assignment now to quit being uneasy and fearful. Fear is the opposite of faith. Sometimes it is very difficult to organize and prepare yourself in such a way that you do not worry. But as the one little boy said, "You can't tell me worry doesn't help.

The things I worry about never happen!" That is the way life is. You go in great courage.

The Lord explained a few things in that interview in 3 Nephi. You ought to read that again and get it a little more perfectly than I have quoted it to you. But the essential is: "What do you want now?"

They said, "We want to know what to name the Church, what to call the Church."

And He said, "Why is it that the people should murmur and dispute because of this thing?

"Have they not read the scriptures, which say ye must take upon you the name of Christ?"

Then He goes on and promises that if they will move in that direction, He will bless the Church. The Lord said, "For my sake."

This matter of the gift of the Holy Ghost and how it is empowered does not happen generally in congregations or in large audiences. Always over the years as I have gone, particularly to priesthood leadership meetings where we are trying to teach the gospel and convey the power of the Holy Ghost, I wonder whether we are getting through.

I went to President Lee once and said I had been out to a conference. I said, "It was not a good experience. I didn't get in."

He knew what I was talking about. He said, "I know you. I know you're good enough. Haven't you learned that if you don't get in, it depends more on them than it does on you?"

I had not thought about that. So it has been an encouragement to me along the way to try to do what the Lord has said.

Now there is the matter of privacy and confidentiality in what we are talking about. You are to teach it openly, but the private experiences you have are best described in the New Testament where Luke was describing the birth of Christ and wrote about Mary. Mary was the one witness that knew all of it. He said as much as he could and then said, "But Mary kept all these things, and pondered them in her heart" (Luke 2:19).

You sisters will have great power in the mission by being just who you are. It is something to call someone away from his profession and his wife goes with him to a land they have never visited, a language they have not heard. And it is the same with the missionaries who go two by two and teach the gospel. They are teenagers! Calling teenagers by the thousands and sending them out into the world is not reasonable. The only thing we have to justify that system is it works. How does it work? Because the power is there.

When it comes to your conveying or sharing that power you have so that they will *feel* it, I want to get to the real center of what I want to talk to you about. You should have the gift of the Holy Ghost with you always. You will find people looking at you as you go down the street because you are different. They want to know how you are different. You cannot very well tell them, but you are. You will have that power.

This matter of doing it one-on-one is the key to it. I know you will have some wonderful sermons that you will give in your district meetings and your zone meetings, but the most power you convey is when you are one-on-one with the missionaries. You can bring them back from going astray. You can lift them when they have fallen down inside of themselves. You have taught them that they can kneel down inside of themselves wherever they are and be prayerful. You teach them that, and you have taught them the greatest gift you can give them.

What are we about in the Church? There are a few lines of verse that I have carried for years:

> *We are blind, until we see*
> *That in the human plan*
> *Nothing is worth the making if*
> *It does not make the man.*
> *Why build these cities glorious*
> *If man unbuilded goes?*

In vain we build the work, unless
The builder also grows.

(Edwin Markham, "Man-Making," *Masterpieces of
Religious Verse*, ed. James Dalton Morrison [1948],
419)

That is what you are doing out there with the missionaries. They
will follow you, and they will love you, and they will forgive you, and
sometimes they will misunderstand. But you will be all right if you
understand what we are about.

The perfect place to get all of this done so it is permanent is with
the family. That is what we are about, trying to focus on the family,
because to get this established in the hearts of the Church, especially the
young people, it comes from the father and the mother in the home.
Often it is a voice that is *felt* rather than *heard*.

You may wonder if your children have or will come to the power
that you think they ought to have. They will. You are earning that for
them. That is one of the blessings you receive in spending whatever
years you are called to be a mission president. If you are looking for reward, the one which might well be worth choosing is that your children
will be redeemed. About all you have to do is be a good wife and a good
mother. You brethren listen to your wife. The heart knows things the
head never can quite understand. Your wife has a tender heart. Do not
stray from the counsel that she gives to you, and you will be all right.

So it is in the home that this takes place. We have been trying to
reduce some of the patterns of activities in the Church to the point
where a father and a mother and their children can be happy at home.
The ultimate effort of everything in the Church is to the end that a
father and a mother and their children can be happy at home. If they
are happy at home, they are spiritually prepared for whatever should be
ahead of them in the world.

We have a missionary boy that is arriving home today from

England. We have another that is going out in three weeks. We have always had to trade one in to get one out. We are enlivened and empowered by their service.

There is a great lesson in Alma. He had a wayward son. He was openly wayward. He actually opposed what his father was trying to do. Then one day he was struck down by an angel. The angel said to him, "If thou wilt of thyself be destroyed, seek no more to destroy the church of God" (Alma 36:9). He was struck down, and in due course, when he came to himself, he had what he needed to have. Alma caused that to be when he was a great distance from his son.

You will have missionaries that you cannot quite get to. You cannot ever be kept away from them because you can pray yourself to them. If you are listening, you will be hearing what you ought to hear about them, and you will be watched over.

One other thing: you ought to know that the Lord loves you. He will make that known to you, and it will be a very private and individual experience, something you cannot explain to anyone else. The only point of contact is if you find someone that you come to know has had exactly the same experience. So you will be all right.

I close with two things: one, bearing a testimony to you. I know that God lives. I know that Jesus is the Christ. I know Jesus. I know the Christ and bear witness of Him.

And then I invoke a blessing upon you, first, of course, as fathers and mothers and as grandparents. This is the most important blessing you could be given.

Incidentally, of less importance but important enough, I bless you as mission presidents and wife-companions. You can reach out as Alma did to his son and bless all of your missionaries. You invoke that power, and as the Lord lives, it will happen. It takes a little faith once in a while to hold onto that which is slow to grow, but if you hold that power, you will know.

I bless you that those you leave behind will be watched over, as well as your personal affairs. The mothers and grandmothers here worrying about the home and the family you leave will have a family of your own when you get there, readymade to take their place.

As you serve, the Lord will bless you. I invoke that blessing upon you and bear witness to you that what you teach is the truth, and the power of that agency will be with you, and the gift of the Holy Ghost, which is given to every soul that comes into the Church, will be manifest in you. You will come to know as surely as you live that there is such a thing as the Holy Ghost, and that the power is there, and that the Spirit can be with you and with them at the same time.

So the Lord bless you, each one of you. You will sort out the things you worry about. Pray about them, and then forget them. Go check later, and you will find that they are all right. That is the way this works. You cannot serve the Lord without receiving a compensatory blessing bigger than your service. You are going to spend now these years full time in the service of your Lord, and He will bless you. He will bless you in the difficulties in the countries that you are going into. You may meet some dangers, but you can do that without being afraid because the power is with you. You exert that power, and miracles will happen. Miracles are not all recorded, and they are not oft talked about, but they happen every day in the Church. You yourself are a miracle. The Church produces every year 130 new mission presidents to go out, willing to leave all of their affairs and go and follow the way of the Master.

I want you to remember the testimony that I have borne that I know the Lord. I know that He lives and that this is His Church. You are His agents in it, you brothers and sisters. This I confirm upon you as a servant of the Lord and in the name of Jesus Christ.

6

TAKE CHARGE OF YOURSELVES

I want to pass to you something I learned from my brother which has been like a shield and a protection to me.

I graduated from flight training and received my silver wings two days before my twentieth birthday. Later I was stationed at Langley Field, Virginia, as copilot on a selected B-24 bomber crew trained to use a new secret weapon—radar.

My brother, Colonel Leon C. Packer, was stationed at the Pentagon in Washington, D. C. A much decorated B-24 pilot, he became a briga-dier general in the Air Force.

While I was at Langley Field, the war in Europe ended, and so we were ordered to the Pacific. I spent a few days with Leon in Washington before shipping out to a military base in California.

While in Washington, Leon told me of things he had learned under fire. He flew from North Africa on raids over southern Europe; very few of those planes returned.

From an address given at general conference, October 2, 1999; see *Ensign*, November 1999, 23–25.

On April 16, 1943, he was captain of a B-24 bomber returning to England after a raid in Europe. His plane, the *Yard Bird,* was heavily damaged by flak and dropped out of formation.

Then they were alone and came under heavy attack from fighters.

His one-page account of that experience says: "Number three engine was smoking and the prop ran away. Number four fuel line was shot out. Right aileron cables and stabilizer cables were shot out. Rudders partially locked. Radio shot out. Extremely large holes in the right wing. Flaps shot out. Entire rear part of the fuselage filled with holes. Hydraulic system shot out. Tail turret out."

A history of the Eighth Air Force, published in 1997, gives a detailed account of that flight written by one of the crew (see Gerald Astor, *Mighty Eighth: The Air War in Europe As Told by the Men Who Fought It).*

With one engine on fire, the other three lost power. They were going down. The alarm bell ordered that they bail out. The bombardier, the only one able to get out, parachuted into the English Channel.

The pilots left their seats and made their way toward the bomb bay to bail out. Suddenly Leon heard an engine cough and sputter. He quickly climbed back to his seat and coaxed enough power from the engines to reach the coast of England. Then the engines failed, and they crashed.

The landing gear was shorn off on the brow of a hill; the plane plowed through trees and crumbled. Dirt filled the fuselage.

Amazingly, though some were terribly wounded, all aboard survived. The bombardier was lost, but he probably saved the lives of the other nine. When smoke poured from the engines and a parachute appeared, the fighters stopped their attack.

As we visited, Leon told me how he was able to hold himself together under fire. He said, "I have a favorite hymn"—and he named it—"and when things got rough I would sing it silently to myself, and there would come a faith and an assurance that kept me on course."

Now, while Leon's experience was dramatic, *the greater value of his lesson came to me later in everyday life* when I faced the same temptations young people and children face now.

As the years passed I found that, while not easy, I could control my thoughts if I made a place for them to go. You can replace thoughts of temptation, anger, disappointment, or fear with better thoughts—with music.

I love the sacred music of the Church. The hymns of the Restoration carry an inspiration and a protection.

I know also some music is spiritually destructive; it's bad and dangerous! Young people, leave it alone!

I know as well why Leon counseled his children, "Remember, the flak is always the heaviest closer to the target."

Thoughts are talks we hold with ourselves. Do you see why the scriptures tell us to "let virtue garnish thy thoughts unceasingly" and promise us that if we do, our "confidence [shall] wax strong in the presence of God; and the doctrine of the priesthood shall distil upon [our] soul[s] as the dews from heaven" and then "the Holy Ghost shall be [our] constant companion"? (D&C 121:45–46).

"The Comforter, which is the Holy Ghost, whom the Father will send in my name, he shall teach you all things, and bring all things to your remembrance, whatsoever I have said unto you" (John 14:26).

The voice of the Spirit is felt rather than heard. You can learn when you are very young how the Holy Ghost works.

The scriptures are full of help on how good can influence your mind and evil control you, if you let it. That struggle will never end. But remember this:

> *All the water in the world,*
> *However hard it tried,*
> *Could never sink the smallest ship*
> *Unless it [gets] inside.*

And all the evil in the world,
The blackest kind of sin,
Can never hurt you the least bit
Unless you let it in.

(Author unknown, in *Best-Loved Poems of the LDS People*, ed. Jack M. Lyon and others [1996], 302)

When you learn to control your thoughts, you will be safe.

One man I know does this: Whenever an unworthy thought tries to enter his mind, he brushes his thumb against his wedding ring. That breaks the circuit and for him becomes an almost automatic way to close out unwanted thoughts and ideas.

I can't refrain from sharing one other thing about that visit with my brother in Washington. He was to take a B-25 bomber to Texas to pick up something and return to Washington the next day. I went with him. That was the only time we flew together.

Many years later I was honored at a banquet by Weber State University, where we both had graduated. He had been a student body officer during his college days. Because I would be in South America during the banquet, he agreed to attend and accept the award in my behalf.

In his acceptance speech he told this story—part of which is true. He said that in Texas we were lined up side by side on the runway ready to take off. He radioed to me and said, "See you upstairs—if you think you can make it!"

Then he told them that after I became a General Authority of the Church, once in a while I would check on his behavior and add, "See you upstairs—if you think you can make it!"

Well, Leon made it. He is now where I hope one day to be.

Young Latter-day Saints, shape up! Face up! Take hold of your lives! Take control of your mind, your thoughts! If you have friends that are not a good influence, make changes, even if you face loneliness, even rejection.

If you have already made bad mistakes, there are ways to fix things up, and eventually it will be as though they never happened.

Sometimes guilt controls our minds and takes us prisoner in our thoughts. How foolish to remain in prison when the door stands open. Now, don't tell yourself that sin really doesn't matter. That won't help; repentance will.

Take charge of yourself. How wonderful to be a young Latter-day Saint in this wonderful, challenging time.

Paul told young Timothy, "Let no man despise thy youth" (1 Timothy 4:12).

And Louisa May Alcott was only fourteen when she wrote:

> *A little kingdom I possess,*
> *Where thoughts and feelings dwell,*
> *And very hard I find the task*
> *Of governing it well; . . .*
>
> *I do not ask for any crown*
> *But that which all may win,*
> *Nor seek to conquer any world;*
> *Except the one within.*
>
> ("My Little Kingdom," in *Louisa May Alcott—Her Girlhood Diary*, ed. Cary Ryan [1993], 8–9)

You can do it—you must do it. Our future depends on you, our children and youth.

I can give you this encouragement: A teacher, trying to explain what a theory is, asked this question: "If you take a letter half the distance to a mailbox and stop, then start over, going half the remaining distance and stop, and repeat the process over and over, theoretically will you ever really get to the mailbox?" One bright student said, "No, but you'll get close enough to mail the letter."

Young people will get close enough to perfection to have a life that is filled with challenges and troubles, with inspiration and happiness and eternal joy.

The Lord promised:

"I will not leave you comfortless: I will come to you" (John 14:18).

"I will tell you in your *mind* and in your *heart,* by the Holy Ghost, which shall come upon you and which shall dwell in your heart. . . .

"This is the spirit of revelation. . . .

"Therefore this is thy gift; apply unto it, and blessed art thou, for it shall deliver you" (D&C 8:2–4; italics added).

7

THE DISEASE OF PROFANITY

A number of years ago I went with a brother to tow in a wrecked car. It was a single-car accident, and the car was demolished; the driver, though unhurt, had been taken to the hospital for treatment of shock and for examination.

The next morning he came asking for his car, anxious to be on his way. When he was shown the wreckage, his pent-up emotions and disappointment, sharpened perhaps by his misfortune, exploded in a long stream of profanity. So obscene and biting were his words that they exposed years of practice with profanity. His words were heard by other customers, among them women, and must have touched their ears like acid.

One of my brothers crawled from beneath the car, where he had been working with a large wrench. He too was upset, and with threatening gestures of the wrench (mechanics will know that a sixteen-inch crescent wrench is a formidable weapon), he ordered the man off the

From an address given at general conference, October 1, 1967; see *Improvement Era*, December 1967, 96–97.

premises. "We don't have to listen to that kind of language here," he said. And the customer left, cursing more obscenely than before.

Much later in the day he reappeared, subdued, penitent, and avoiding everyone else, he found my brother.

"I have been in the hotel room all day," he said, "lying on the bed tormented. I can't tell you how utterly ashamed I am for what happened this morning. My conduct was inexcusable. I have been trying to think of some justification, and I can think of only one thing. In all my life, never, not once, have I been told that my language was not acceptable. I have always talked that way. You were the first one who ever told me that my language was out of order."

The Havoc of Profanity

Isn't it interesting that a man could grow to maturity, the victim of such a vile habit, and never meet a protest? How tolerant we have become, and how quickly we are moving. A generation ago writers of newspapers, editors of magazines, and particularly the producers of motion pictures carefully censored profane and obscene words.

All that has now changed. It began with the novel. Writers, insisting that they must portray life as it is, began to put into the mouths of their characters filthy, irreverent expressions. These words on the pages of books came before the eyes of all ages and imprinted themselves on the minds of our youth.

Carefully (we are always led carefully), profanity has inched and nudged and pushed its way relentlessly into the motion picture and the magazine, and now even newspapers print verbatim comments the likes of which would have been considered intolerable a generation ago.

"Why not show life as it is?" they ask. They even say it is hypocritical to do otherwise. "If it is real," they say, "why hide it? You can't censor that which is real!"

Why hide it? Why protest against it? Many things that are real are not right. Disease germs are real, but must we therefore spread them?

A pestilent infection may be real, but ought we to expose ourselves to it? Those who argue that so-called "real life" is license must remember that where there's an *is,* there's an *ought.* Frequently, what is and what ought to be are far apart. When *is* and *ought* come together, an ideal is formed. The reality of profanity does not argue for the toleration of it.

Controls for Discipline

Like the man in the shop, many of us may never have been told how serious an offense profanity can be. Ere we know it we are victims of a vile habit—and the servant to our tongue. The scriptures declare:

"Behold, we put bits in the horses' mouths, that they may obey us; and we turn about their whole body.

"Behold also the ships, which though they be so great, and are driven of fierce winds, yet are they turned about with a very small helm, whithersoever the governor listeth.

"Even so the tongue is a little member, and boasteth great things. . . .

"For every kind of beasts, and of birds, and of serpents, and of things in the sea, is tamed, and hath been tamed of mankind:

"But the tongue can no man tame; it is an unruly evil, full of deadly poison.

"Therewith bless we God, even the Father; and therewith curse we men, which are made after the similitude of God.

"Out of the same mouth proceedeth blessing and cursing. My brethren, these things ought not so to be" (James 3:3–5, 7–10).

Habit Patterns for Discipline

There is something on this subject I would tell young people who are forming the habit patterns of their lives. Take, for example, the young athlete and his coach. I single out the coach, for to him, as to few others, a boy will yield his character to be molded.

Young athlete, it is a great thing to aspire for a place on the team. A young man like you is willing to give anything to belong. Your coach becomes an ideal to you; you want his approval and to be like him. But remember, if that coach is in the habit of swearing, if he directs the team with profane words or corrects and disciplines the athletes with obscenities, that is a weakness in him, not a strength. That is nothing to be admired nor to be copied. It is a flaw in his character. While it may not seem a big one, through that flaw can seep contamination sufficient to weaken and destroy the finest of characters, as a disease germ can lay low the well-framed, athletically strong, physical body.

Coach, there are men in the making on the practice field. Haven't you learned that when a boy wants so much to succeed, if he hasn't pleased you, that silence is more powerful than profanity?

While this counsel may apply to other professions, I single you out, coach, because of your unparalleled power of example (and perhaps because the lesson is needed).

Better Than Profanity

There is no need for any of us to use profanity. Realize that you are more powerful in expression without it. I give you two examples.

Sir Winston Churchill, in his postwar account of the struggle with Nazism, introduced the most revolting character in recent centuries without a profane adjective: "Thereafter mighty forces were adrift, the void was open, and into that void after a pause there strode a maniac of ferocious genius, the repository and expression of the most virulent hatreds that have ever corroded the human breast—Corporal Hitler" (*The Gathering Storm* [1948], 10).

Nobody needs to profane!

You may argue that we are not all Winston Churchills. Therefore, this next example is within the reach of most everyone.

On one occasion, two of our children were at odds. A four-year-old boy, irritated beyond restraint by an older brother but with no vocabulary of profanity to fall back upon, forced out his lower lip and satisfied the moment with two words: "You ugly!"

Nobody needs to swear!

Because of little protest, like the man in the shop, any of us may have fallen victim to the habit of profanity. If this has been your misfortune, I know a way that you can break the habit quickly. This is what I suggest you do: Make an agreement with someone not in your family but someone who works closest with you. Offer to pay him $1.00 or $2.00, even $5.00, each time he hears you swear. For less than $50.00 you can break the habit. Smile if you will, but you will find it is a very practical and powerful device.

Control of Emotions

Now, there is a compelling reason beyond courtesy or propriety or culture for breaking such a habit. Profanity is more than just untidy language, for when we profane, we relate to low and vulgar words the most sacred of all names. I wince when I hear the name of the Lord so used, called upon in anger, in frustration, in hatred.

This is more than just a name we deal with. This relates to spiritual authority and power and lies at the very center of Christian doctrine.

The Lord said, "Therefore, whatsoever ye shall do, ye shall do it in my name" (3 Nephi 27:7).

In the Church that Jesus Christ established, all things are done in His name. Prayers are said, children blessed, testimonies borne, sermons preached, ordinances performed, sacrament administered, the infirm anointed, graves dedicated.

What a mockery it then becomes when we use that sacred name profanely.

If you need some feeling for the seriousness of the offense, next time you hear such an expression or you are tempted to use one yourself, substitute the name of your mother, or your father, or your child, or your own name. Perhaps then the insulting and degrading implications will be borne into you, to have a name you revere so used. Perhaps then you will understand the third commandment.

"Thou shalt not take the name of the Lord thy God in vain; for the

Lord will not hold him guiltless that taketh his name in vain" (Exodus 20:7).

Reverence and Worship in His Name

However common irreverence and profanity become, they are nonetheless wrong. We teach our children so. In The Church of Jesus Christ of Latter-day Saints, we revere His name. We worship in His name; we love Him.

He said: "Behold, verily, verily, I say unto you, ye must watch and pray always lest ye enter into temptation; for Satan desireth to have you, that he may sift you as wheat.

"Therefore ye must always pray unto the Father *in my name;*

"And whatsoever ye shall ask the Father *in my name,* which is right, believing that ye shall receive, behold it shall be given unto you.

"Pray in your families unto the Father, *always in my name,* that your wives and your children may be blessed" (3 Nephi 18:18–21; italics added).

The authority to use His name has been restored. The disease of profanity, now in epidemic proportions, is spreading across the land, and so, in His name, we pray that a purity of heart might descend upon us, for out of the abundance of the heart the mouth speaketh.

8

FOLLOW THE RULE

I remember very vividly the first time I was in Laie, Hawaii, years ago. I think I'll mention one or two of the circumstances surrounding my visit by way of illustrating something I learned from that experience. The date is easy to remember because it was a signal date in world history—14 August 1945.

Some time earlier than that I had been in military training in the United States. World War II was in full course. A few months earlier Germany had surrendered, and shortly after that we left for California, heading into the Pacific theater of war.

While I was at a base in California, I had my patriarchal blessing. I hadn't had one when I was home. I went to a patriarch that I had never seen before, and would not see again for twenty years, and received what Brother LeGrand Richards has described as "a page from your book of possibilities." That became a very important element in my life and in the experiences I had in the Pacific.

We sailed from Seattle at night, for security reasons. The ship was

From an address given at Brigham Young University–Hawaii, January 14, 1977.

very crowded—there were six hundred men on deck, besides all those who were accommodated below deck—moving, as we were then, large numbers of troops into the war zone. As we boarded that ship that night and as I went to my bunk, I felt it was something of an end and a beginning in my life. I made a firm resolution that night that should I come back from the war—and I expected that I would come back—I would know for sure that the gospel was true. I believed it was true; but I determined that, whatever awaited us, when I returned I would know. As part of the commitment to that, I began my first reading of the Book of Mormon. I had "read" it before, but this time I determined to *read* it, and there is a difference.

We landed at Honolulu and then went to Kauai, where, at Barking Sands near Kekaha, there was an airbase. We were there for some weeks, and I desired greatly to see the temple. I didn't have a recommend, and I couldn't go into the temple, but I wanted to be on the temple grounds. I was about nineteen at the time and had just graduated from pilot training. A USO group, a group of entertainers—comedians and some other movie figures—had been to Kauai to entertain the troops. They were going back to Oahu by plane. I managed to get aboard that plane to Honolulu and hitchhiked to Laie to spend part of a day on the temple grounds.

It was late that afternoon when I returned to Honolulu. I was in a little Chinese curio shop buying a small carved box for my sister when pandemonium broke loose. Someone came in and spoke in very great excitement to the proprietor of the shop, in Chinese, I assumed. He forthwith pushed me from the shop and pulled the blind down. Then I saw people pouring from the buildings into the streets, and the cars all stopped. It had just been announced that the Japanese had surrendered—the war was over. I thought, "We can go home. It's all over." That, however, was not to be.

A few days later, on another ship, we set sail for the Philippines, to be part of the occupation forces. In the course of the next year we moved from the Philippines to Okinawa, then to Tokyo, and finally, more than a year later, I returned home. During the interim I became acquainted with the revelations and the scriptures. I read the Book of Mormon and read it again—and again.

I would like to focus for just a moment on the scriptures. By way of introduction I'd like to quote from the New Testament, from Timothy, words written by Paul to Timothy. They might have been taken from the front page of today's newspaper; they're that pertinent. It's a familiar scripture that applies particularly to those who are young.

"This know also, that in the last days perilous times shall come.

"For men shall be lovers of their own selves, covetous, boasters, proud, blasphemers, disobedient to parents, [imagine reading that in the scriptures from ancient times!], unthankful, unholy,

"Without natural affection [imagine reading that in scriptures from ancient times], trucebreakers, false accusers, incontinent, fierce, despisers of those that are good,

"Traitors, heady, highminded, lovers of pleasures more than lovers of God; [and then, strangely enough,]

"Having a form of godliness, but denying the power thereof: from such turn away" (2 Timothy 3:1–5).

That was the prophetic description of what our day would be—all of those things. It's negative, as you contemplate it. Think that all of these things surround us.

It wasn't until recently that I happened to glance down the page and make a connection I never had before. That's often the case with scriptures, isn't it? Though we think we have command of them, they're a continued revelation. At the bottom of that page I read this:

"But evil men and seducers shall wax worse and worse, deceiving, and being deceived."

And then, here's the answer for all of us to that which is ominous and negative and frightening:

"But continue thou in the things which thou hast learned and hast been assured of, knowing of whom thou hast learned them;

"And that from a child thou hast known the holy scriptures, which are able to make thee wise unto salvation through faith which is in Christ Jesus.

"All scripture is given by inspiration of God, and is profitable for doctrine, for reproof, for correction, for instruction in righteousness:

"That the man of God may be perfect, throughly furnished unto all good works" (2 Timothy 3:13–17).

On the one hand we have the ominous, frightening, prophetic declaration of what we face in our generation, and following it the antidote or the immunization from it in that we have the scriptures.

I would like to take a phrase from what we've just read to illustrate something, and then I will share some specific counsel.

"But evil men and seducers shall wax worse and worse, deceiving, and being deceived.

"But continue thou in the things which thou hast learned and hast been assured of [and this is the phrase I want to emphasize:] *knowing of whom thou hast learned them.*"

I repeat: "Knowing of whom thou hast learned them."

I now turn to the forty-second section of the Doctrine and Covenants, verse 11:

"Again I say unto you, that it shall not be given to any one to go forth to preach my gospel, or to build up my church, except he be ordained by some one who has authority, and it is known to the church that he has authority and has been regularly ordained by the heads of the church."

In our day it is manifestly impossible on this earth for someone to get off a plane somewhere and represent himself, for instance, as a member of the Council of the Twelve and proceed to give instruction or to perform ordinations that would be counterfeit. This couldn't be done. We're too well known in a very interesting way.

I'd like to tell you of an experience that happened just a short time ago. My oldest son took his little family to tithing settlement. When they went into the bishop's office, there was a picture of all of the General Authorities. Our tiny granddaughter noticed the picture and got all excited and said, "Oh, Grandpa, Grandpa!" My daughter-in-law lifted her up, and she pointed to Brother McConkie!

Some time ago my wife and I were coming home from New Zealand. We had left Auckland about midnight and landed in Papeete, Tahiti, to change planes in the wee hours of the morning. We had an hour or two to spend and were waiting for our flight to come in. A Pan American plane landed, and we were watching that plane taxi in. I didn't know where it was from or where it was going, but I said to my wife, "I will know someone on that flight." It was just a flight out in the Pacific in the wee hours of a Monday morning.

I went out and stood by the gate. I knew one man as he got off. Four other people came up and said, "You're Brother Packer, aren't you?" That's a handicap sometimes to us personally, but there's a great protection in that for the Church.

Some time ago I was with President Kimball in New York. We had gone to tape an interview that was going to go on the CBS nation-wide broadcast. It was a beautiful Saturday morning in April and we decided to walk up Fifth Avenue to the mission home. Thousands of people were out walking, and President Kimball said, "Look at all of these people—and they're all ours. They all should have the gospel, and not a one of them knows us. All of them are strangers to us," he said.

"I know how we can find someone we know," I said.

"How can we find them?" he asked.

We were passing a little French restaurant with tables sitting out on the sidewalk. I said, "We can just step over there and order coffee, and someone will find us in a hurry!"

Just as I had said that in a joking way, I heard the words: "Brother

Kimball! Brother Kimball!" Out of the crowd came the wife of a stake president!

The point I make is that this phrase from Timothy strikes me as being monumentally important: "But continue thou in the things which thou hast learned and hast been assured of, knowing of whom thou hast learned them." In the pattern of constituted authority in the Church, we always know where revelation comes from. Revelation is always vertical. There is no horizontal revelation in the Church. It is all vertical. A bishop will get no revelation from a fellow bishop, or a stake president from a fellow stake president; but a bishop will receive it from his stake president, and his stake president from the general officers of the Church.

In your youth you can learn that the scriptures are powerful, that they're righteous; that in this Church we learn the scriptures, that we accept them, that we determine to live by them. Learn that there is a constituted authority—that our leaders are ordained by those who are in authority, and it is known throughout the Church. Nothing is done in the corner where there might be room for doubt or confusion or misunderstanding. We all have the right to go before the Lord to appeal in prayer and to receive inspiration and revelation for ourselves, so that each of us will know.

One of the things the scriptures do is to make it very clear that we're to follow the prophets. In the Doctrine and Covenants, section after section states, "I the Lord am speaking," or "It is I, God, who speaks," and so on. Those declarations show that there is no doubt who is speaking.

Now I would like to touch upon another bit of counsel from those who are ordained (and it is known to the world that they are ordained). This counsel has direct and specific application to those who are scattered across the earth, learning the gospel in their own tongues and culture and facing the question: "Where can I serve?" The counsel has been, and the counsel is, that you're to serve among your people, to bless your people now. Can everyone who lives in foreign lands and places removed from the headquarters of the Church do that? There may be valid exceptions, of course.

But we need to be careful with the idea of "exceptions." On one occasion when I was president of the New England Mission, we were holding a Relief Society conference of several hundred women. Our Relief Society president was a convert. We were trying to get our sewing circles and gossip festivals turned into Relief Societies. We were setting the standards for Relief Society, and this lovely sister was told to teach the sisters what a Relief Society should be.

At this Relief Society conference she was explaining that the Relief Society would no longer be held on Sunday, that they would hold it on weekdays so that they could have sewing and activities and so on. A woman stood up in the audience and defied her and said, "You don't understand. Things are different up in Vermont. This is different, we are an exception. We can't do that. You must make an exception."

The Relief Society president was quite puzzled at this confrontation. She turned around and looked at me, pleading for help. I thought she was doing pretty well, so I motioned for her to proceed. She did, and what she said next was so profound that I told her after the meeting I would be quoting that across the world, since I was sure it came by inspiration. For she stood there, frightened and puzzled, for a few minutes while that defiant woman, who was something of a ringleader representing a faction, kept talking for a minute, reemphasizing that they were an exception. Then Sister Baker quietly but firmly said, "Dear sister, we'd like not to take care of the exception first. We'll see to the rule first, and then we'll take care of the exception."

Now, what are you to do in your lives? Accommodate the rule first! If you're to be an exception, or if others are to be an exception, that will become obvious in the inspiration that comes. But there is great power and great safety in holding to the scriptures and having an abounding obedience to our constituted priesthood authority. We are able to pray and receive revelation on our own and then to obediently say, "Lord, I don't ask to be an exception."

The counsel for us to gather to our own people is counsel from the prophets, who are known as the constituted authority, having been ordained and known to the Church. Now, there's great importance in following that counsel. Sometimes when we go out to seek our fortunes in places far from home, we think that we are an exception and that there are so many more opportunities available in other lands.

We can make obedience our rule—and not the exception—even when it goes against all our plans. I remember from my college days the report of an eminent historian. He had gone to southern Utah to gather some of the local historical facts. He had looked up the oldest man in the community—a man in his nineties. In the interview he suggested to the man that he was living in what might be termed "a forsaken little place on the desert." He asked him, "How did you get here?"

The man told him that he had been called there on a mission.

He said, "Who called you here on the mission?"

The man said, "The president of the Church" (I think it was probably John Taylor or Wilford Woodruff).

The historian said, "But you've stayed here all your life. Why didn't you ever go back?" The old man did not have much of an answer, and the historian pressed the point, asking, "Why didn't you go back to a better place?"

Then tears came to the old man's eyes, and he said, "No, I could not go back. I was called on a mission, and I have not been released." And then from the porch of this humble little house he pointed over to a sagebrush hill where there were headstones and said, "I'll go there before I'll go back."

I think of the young couple in the early days of our missionary effort in the Pacific islands who were sent on a mission to Samoa—a young man and his wife. This young married couple arrived in Samoa on a ship, and as they were being put ashore in a small boat, the hardened seamen stood at the rails and wept over the young couple going to what they termed a "godforsaken place." There are graves in Samoa, as there are on the other South Pacific islands, of missionaries who were "forgotten" but not by the Lord. There is a conviction and a dedication that we can have, and that we ought to have, to be obedient.

We can do as Samuel did. Remember the story of Eli and Samuel? Eli, the old prophet, had the boy Samuel to train. The little boy came to him and said, "Somebody keeps calling to me at night."

The old prophet said, "What do they say?"

The boy said, "They just call my name: Samuel. I get up and look around, but there's nobody there."

The wise old prophet, teaching this young lad, who himself would be a prophet one day, said, "When that happens again, your answer should be, 'Speak, Lord, for thy servant heareth'" (see 1 Samuel 3:3–10).

If we could build that in our lives—"Speak, Lord, for thy servant heareth"—then we would find ourselves among our own people doing what we ought to do, living as we ought to live. The glitter of the enticements of other places would not persuade us.

I have a lingering, sensitive, prophetic idea that those who obediently follow the prophet will live to know a stability and a fulness and a plenty in their own lands that by comparison they now seem deprived of economically. They will have far more of what matters most than they would have if they should go elsewhere seeking their fortune.

When you come to find that which matters most, you will always find in the long run that to be the rule and not the exception is to see the fulness of life. Should there be exceptions, the Lord will designate those in an unmistakable way.

I would remind you of that Relief Society woman's near-scriptural statement: "We'd like not to take care of the exceptions first. We'd like to follow the rule first, and then we'll take care of the exceptions."

I was with President Spencer W. Kimball once some years ago

when, in a small group, he told the story of his courtship and marriage to Camilla Eyring. They knew one another for only a short time. I'm even hesitant to say how short the time was before their marriage. He told of meeting this beautiful young schoolteacher who had come to the community, and in the course of a few weeks they were married. After hearing this, one young man in the group later said, "Well, if President Kimball can find somebody and be sure in that short of a time, I guess I can do that."

Someone else replied, "My boy, before you think that applies to you, you ought to be very sure you have the inspiration and power that are present in the beginnings of an Apostle."

You may not be the exception. We counsel in the Church, for instance, that we ought to be old enough before we marry and we ought to know one another before we're married. Our courtships ought to be adequate. You may pick out a couple—he was eighteen and she was seventeen when they married—and see how happy and successful they've been. Yes, an exception! For every exception we can show you tens and hundreds, and I suppose thousands, who were not happy. Young people should plan to marry within their own culture. This counsel is good, and I hope our branch presidents are paying attention to it. The counsel is good.

Now, someone may say, "Well, I've never heard that in general conference." I remember once that President Harold B. Lee gave a talk at BYU, and he told me that he felt some unusual inspiration in that talk and gave emphasis to a point that he had not intended to discuss. A few days later one of the professors from BYU called at his office and said, "Brother Lee, I was very interested in your talk. I was very interested in one point particularly."

Brother Lee said, "Yes, I was quite interested too."

The professor said, "Would you mind citing the reference and the authority for that?"

Brother Lee thought for a few minutes and said, "Yes, the reference for that is Elder Harold B. Lee of the Council of the Twelve Apostles, speaking at a devotional assembly at BYU," and then he gave the date of his sermon. The point I make, simply, is this: It isn't a question of who said it or when; the question is whether it is true.

Of course, we always have the test. Somebody said, "No matter how tall your grandpa is, we've all got to do our own growing." Everybody in this Church may go to his own sacred grove to ask what is true. That is what happened to me in the Pacific. I came back a different man because I came to know that God lives and that Jesus is the Christ. I know that there are great powers intervening in our lives.

I think I will mention a personal experience. While I was stationed in Tokyo, on one occasion we were assigned to take a B-17 bomber and go down to Saipan Island and then on to Guam, if necessary, to get a beacon light. I was an operations officer, and we needed a beacon light at the base. We left Tokyo, heading south into the Pacific. Because the war was just over, air flight safety was not put together as it is now. We did not know that there was forming, out in the central Pacific, a typhoon of major proportions.

Now, Pacific islands from airplanes are very difficult to see; clouds look like islands and vice versa. I remember the navigator said, "If we're on course, we should be over Iwo Jima soon." He began counting: "Ten, nine, eight," and so on, and when he counted "zero," we tipped the plane and looked down through broken clouds, and directly below us was Iwo Jima. We were right on course. We kidded him about being an expert.

Several hours later he said, "We're off course. Something's wrong!" We dropped down through the cloud cover. There were terrible winds. The ocean was white with waves. He said, "I don't know where we are." Then, of course, to add melodrama to the drama, the radios went out. There we were!

We began flying a "square search." Lost pilots don't just fly around aimlessly. They fly a definite pattern so that they know they're covering new territory and not just flying in circles. We flew a long course on the compass. The other pilot said, "Let's turn." For some reason I said, "Hold it just a minute." We were just a few thousand feet above the water. Suddenly I could see a long line of white waves, and we pulled up over some rocks sticking out of the ocean. We knew then that somewhere nearby was an island. We had no idea whether we were over the rocks south of it or north of it. We made a prayerful turn, and in about five or ten minutes on our short-range radio we could hear voices. Soon we pulled over Tinian Island where there was an airfield. As we landed the B-17 and were taxiing down the runway, one by one the engines went off. We were out of gas.

During the last hour of that flight, when I sat there wondering if we would or if we wouldn't make it, my patriarchal blessing kept coming to my mind. It said, "You will be warned of danger, and if you heed those warnings, you will be privileged to return to your loved ones." I thought, "Well, I've tried." I sat there thinking, "The gospel's true, and what else matters? That prophetic declaration will see us safely through this, and if it doesn't, we're in the hands of the Lord now."

Things are not always easy when we receive counsel, whether the counsel is to serve among our own people or whether it is counsel to marry within our own cultural backgrounds. Always there is a decision. Always we can say, "We're an exception." But I say, in the words of that Relief Society sister, "As for me, I'm going to follow the rule first; and then, should there be an exception, perhaps that will be made known."

Elder Marion G. Romney said once, "I don't know any more certainly right now that God lives than I knew when I was a missionary boy in Australia." There was one difference, though, he said: "Then I came to know that the Lord lives. Since then I have come to know the Lord."

I bear witness that God lives, that Jesus is the Christ. I bear witness that prophetic, apostolic powers are on this earth. That power rests

75

upon this Church and kingdom. You and I have the privilege and the obligation of bearing this kingdom away in such fashion that all mankind will be served by it. God grant that we might be worthy and able and inspired.

PART THREE

PRIESTHOOD

9

A PRIESTHOOD OF PREPARATION

I have seven sons, and I have learned a great deal from them and have had to depend a great deal upon them. Sometimes we have had another holder of the Melchizedek Priesthood at home; often we have not. Our elders have been on missions, or they are married, so the priesthood in our home has been Aaronic Priesthood. I am away a great deal and am very grateful for our young sons who hold the priesthood.

I want to address the subject of this priesthood and tell you a story or two from our family experience. Several years ago our sons would spend their time during the summer on their grandfather's ranch. Twelve years ago our son had a horse. It had been given to him when it was born. It had been running with a wild herd of horses on the ranch. It was now two years old and was ready to be broken to ride. Early one summer we went to the ranch. It took all day to get the horses into the corral. Finally we had his horse in a chute and put a heavy halter on it. We put a big rope on it and tied it to a big post. "Now the horse must

From an address given at a Brazil area conference priesthood session, November 4, 1978; see *New Era*, May 1979, 42–44.

stay there for two or three days," I told my son, "until it quits fighting the rope, until it settles down." We worked with it during the morning, and then we went in to eat. My son hurried with his meal and then went out to his horse. He was fourteen. He loved that horse.

Just as we finished the meal, I heard a noise, and I heard him shout. I knew what had happened. He had untied the horse. I had told him not to, but he was going to work with it. In order to hold the horse, he wrapped the rope around his wrist. As I came out the door, I saw that horse run by. My son was running with great big steps, pulled by the horse; and then he fell. If the horse had turned right, it would have gone out the gate into the mountains. It turned left and was cornered in two fences. While it was trying to find its way out, I got the rope off my boy's wrist, and the end of the rope around the post. He was bruised but not badly hurt.

In a little while we had the horse tied up again, and we sat down for a father-and-son lesson. I said to him this: "My boy, if you are ever going to control that horse, you will have to use something besides your muscles. The horse is bigger than you are; it is stronger than you are. Someday you can ride that horse, but it will have to be trained. You cannot train it with your muscles. It is bigger than you are; it is stronger than you are; and it is wild."

Two years later we went to the ranch in the spring. This horse had been running all winter with the herd. We went to find it. We found the herd of horses down by the river. I knew if we went too close, they would run. So this boy and his sister took a bucket with some oats and walked quietly to the edge of the meadow. The horses began to move away slowly. Then he whistled, and his horse came out of the herd and trotted up to my boy. He had learned a great lesson. Much had happened in those two years. He had used more than his muscles.

After that near accident had happened, he was frightened. He had disobeyed. And he had said, "Dad, what should we do?" And I said,

"This is the way we will do it. And one day that horse will run up to you." He had been prepared and had learned a great lesson.

The Aaronic Priesthood is the preparatory priesthood. It is the lesser priesthood. Preparatory for what? It is to prepare young men to hold the Melchizedek Priesthood. It is to prepare young men for life. It is to train them to be leaders. It is to train them in obedience. It is to train them to get control of things that are bigger than they are. It is to show them how to use more than their muscles.

Now, when a young man is ordained a deacon at age twelve, he joins a quorum. Oh, what a marvelous blessing it is to belong to a quorum. All of his life he will belong to a quorum: the deacons quorum with twelve members; the teachers quorum with twenty-four members; the priests quorum with forty-eight members. Then, if he is faithful and worthy, he will be ordained to the Melchizedek Priesthood, or the higher priesthood. The Aaronic Priesthood is to prepare us for that, to make us worthy of holding the Melchizedek Priesthood. We are to learn how to do things in the same way we will do them when we hold the Melchizedek Priesthood.

Let me tell you about this boy again. Now he is married. He has graduated with a degree in engineering and he is leaving to go away to a big city. He and his wife are nervous—a new job, a new home, away from the family.

He told me these two experiences. He worked in a large room with a lot of engineers. After he had been there for two months, he was getting things ready so that he could leave his work on time. We had taught him to arrive at work a little early and to stay a little after time, to do a little extra. But this day he wanted to get away right on time. One of the other engineers asked him where he was going. "What are you in such a hurry for?" "Well, we are going to a dinner tonight." "What kind of a dinner?" "It's a quorum dinner. We are taking our wives to a special dinner and a social." The other engineer shook his head. "I don't understand you. I've been here two years; I don't know anybody yet. Me and my wife are just still to ourselves. You've been here for two months. Already you've been invited to dinner."

The next experience. One day one of the engineers asked if he would help him move. "We found a better apartment. Saturday we are going to move. I need some help. Will you help me?" Our son said, "Why, of course." And then his wife made some bread for them and prepared a meal. He helped them move. Then he said this: "Dad, I've been thinking about that. He hardly knows me. I hardly knew who he was." And he said, "If I'm the one that was the closest to him, the one he would dare to ask help him move, he doesn't have anybody." And he said, "Look what I have."

When he arrived at the new city, they went to church. He went to *his* quorum; he belonged the day he walked in. A quorum—to sustain one another, to help one another. A quorum of the priesthood. Boys of the Aaronic Priesthood can begin to prepare now. They are trained to help others: to gather the fast offerings; to take care of other assignments, the sacrament, home teaching; to be trained to help others. Why? They belong to a quorum. A quorum. The word *quorum* is a marvelous word. In the Church, quorums have never yet fully come into their own.

It is a tremendous honor to belong to a quorum. To be called to preside over a quorum is a signal responsibility. To be called as the secretary of a quorum, or to teach a quorum, is a tremendous responsibility. Do you know where the word *quorum* comes from? It isn't in the Old Testament or the New Testament. It comes from ancient Rome. When they would form a commission of great importance to perform a great work, they would appoint the members of this commission. And they would send them their certificate. And on that certificate the word *quorum* would appear. It would tell what the commission was going to do, how important it was, that great men were being chosen, and then it would contain these words: *Quorum vos unum,* meaning "you are to be one."

What a tremendous opportunity to belong to a quorum. It means you can learn to control life. You can learn to be in charge, to take care of your life and to assist others. I am grateful to have held the Aaronic Priesthood and to still hold it. I am more grateful that my sons have held it and grateful that you can hold it. The priesthood is a great opportunity.

10

IT IS THE POSITION THAT COUNTS

I would like to tell of a little incident that happened to a great member of the Church in Germany, Karl G. Maeser, a great educator, a doctor of education, a man of great dignity and wisdom. It was he who founded Brigham Young University.

Under the direction of President Brigham Young, Brother Maeser went to Provo with the simple instruction that he was to found the university and to teach not even the multiplication tables without the Spirit of God. Beyond that, Brigham Young said, "Good luck and God bless you." Brother Maeser had been converted here in Europe. This man of great dignity and prestige was a very humble man, and his attitude seems to me to characterize what we should be as holders of the priesthood.

I mention two incidents. On one occasion he was going with a group of young missionaries across the Alps. They were crossing a high mountain pass on foot. There were long sticks stuck into the snow of

From an address given at a Dortmund, Germany, area conference priesthood session, August 6, 1976; see *New Era*, June 1977, 50–52.

the glacier to mark the path so that travelers could find their way safely across the glacier and down the mountain on the other side.

When they reached the summit, Brother Maeser wanted to teach the young elders a lesson. He stopped at the pinnacle of the mountain and pointed to those sticks that they had followed. And he said, "Brethren, behold the priesthood of God. They are just common old sticks, but it's the position that counts. Follow them and you will surely be safe. Stray from them and you will surely be lost." And so it is in the Church. We are called to leadership positions and given the power of the priesthood. And we are just common old sticks, but the position we are given counts. It is separate and apart from us, but while we hold it, we hold it.

Now in our wards and in our branches and in our stakes, the Lord calls to positions of leadership the brethren who are there. None of them is perfect. But they hold the office, and we are to be obedient to them.

When Brother Maeser was going to Zion, he stopped in London, where he was called on a mission and told he wouldn't be going on to Zion for a long period of time. That was a great disappointment to him. And there was a great test connected with it. He had been the headmaster of a school, a professor of great dignity. When he walked into a class, all of the students stood up out of respect for this distinguished scholar.

He felt because of his social position there were some things he couldn't do. He wouldn't carry packages in the street, for instance; that was below his station in life. He wouldn't carry a suitcase; that was below his station in life. Wasn't he Herr Dr. Professor, the headmaster, a man of great dignity? And his test came from two humble missionaries. They were going to leave London and go up north to do their missionary work.

The young elder said, "Brother Maeser, you take your suitcase and meet us at the station, and we will meet you there and go on the train." Brother Maeser paced his room all day—to think that they had told him to carry a suitcase through the streets. He worried about it, he talked to his wife about it, and she counseled him, and finally he said to himself and his wife, "The elders have told me to do it, and they are presiding over me, and I will do it." And he took his suitcase and walked to the station.

Now that is just a little thing, but it was almost like Gethsemane for Dr. Maeser to submit himself to the leadership of these young elders.

There is something of the spirit of the priesthood there. When I was a little fellow, I can remember once having an evening meal at home. Father was having a conversation with Mother. Mother had been shopping in town that day. Father said, "Did you get the things you wanted in town?"

"Yes," she said, "I got everything I wanted."

And he asked, "Well, did anything special happen to you in town?"

And my mother said, "Oh, yes. I met the bishop!"

Mother had met the bishop. Now, she saw him every week. And it was just Brother Dredge who ran the seed store. But he was the bishop.

Now, the conversation didn't go like this:

"Anything special in town?"

"No, nothing."

"See anybody you know?"

"Oh, nobody special. Oh, I did see the bishop."

No, not with my mother. She hadn't just seen the bishop. She had seen the *Bishop.*

Do you understand? Somehow there was born into my soul an idea that my mother knew that the bishop was a servant of the Lord. And it wasn't just Brother Dredge. I don't know that we have a perfect bishop in the Church. Or a perfect stake president. Or even a perfect General Authority. I know many of them are near perfection. But they are called to preside over us.

Now, when someone is called to the position to preside over us, we become obedient, just as Brother Maeser did. The great Herr Dr.

Professor said of the young elders, "They have been called to preside over me, and they have told me to do it, and I will do it."

I learned a great lesson. This Church is run by revelation. It comes to those who have the responsibility to preside. I am not sure you could get me to vote against a proposition presented by my presiding authority. I'd be very careful. He might just be a common old stick, but it would be the position that counts.

So in our home, we don't talk about the bishop. We talk about the *bishop*. We don't just have a bishop. We have a *bishop*. And we have *home teachers*. And we have a *stake president*. And in this Church we have a *prophet*. It's the position that counts. The power and the authority go together.

11

THE BISHOP AND
HIS COUNSELORS

Years ago I served on a stake high council with Emery Wight. For ten years Emery had served as bishop of rural Harper Ward. His wife, Lucille, became our stake Relief Society president.

Lucille told me that one spring morning a neighbor called at her door and asked for Emery. She told him that he was out plowing. The neighbor then spoke with great concern. Earlier that morning he had passed the field and noticed Emery's team of horses standing in a half-finished furrow with the reins draped over the plow. Emery was nowhere in sight. The neighbor thought nothing of it until much later when he passed the field again, and the team had not moved. He climbed the fence and crossed the field to the horses. Emery was nowhere to be found. The neighbor hurried to the house to check with Lucille.

Lucille calmly replied, "Oh, don't be alarmed. No doubt someone is in trouble and came to get the bishop."

From an address given at general conference, April 4, 1999; see *Ensign*, May 1999, 57–63.

The image of that team of horses standing for hours in the field symbolizes the dedication of the bishops in the Church and of the counselors who stand by their side. Every bishop and every counselor, figuratively speaking, leaves his team standing in an unfinished furrow when someone needs help.

I have passed that field many times over the years. It is a reminder of the sacrifice and the service of those called to serve in bishoprics of wards and of their wives and families, without whose help they could not serve.

Recently, very early on a Sunday morning, I stood in that field. I looked up toward the home where Emery and Lucille reared their children and to the foothills beyond. As a boy, with other Scouts, I left that home with Bishop Wight. We hiked into the hills, with Emery teaching us every step of the way.

"A bishop," Paul wrote to Timothy, "must be blameless, the husband of one wife, vigilant, sober, of good behaviour, given to hospitality, apt to teach" (1 Timothy 3:2).

Those words *apt to teach* have special meaning. *Apt* means "inclined, ready, prepared."

In all the world there is nothing quite like the office of bishop in The Church of Jesus Christ of Latter-day Saints. Except for parents, the bishop has the best opportunity to teach and to cause to be taught the things that matter most. And a bishop has the remarkable opportunity to teach parents about their responsibility; then he must allow them time to teach their children.

The bishop is responsible for the young men of the Aaronic Priesthood and for the young women as well. He receives and accounts for tithes and offerings. He is responsible for the temporal affairs of the Church, to seek out the poor, and he has many other duties.

The bishop is "to judge his people by the testimony of the just, and *by the assistance of his counselors,* according to the laws of the kingdom which are given by the prophets of God" (D&C 58:18; italics added).

He is to judge them as to their worthiness to receive the ordinances and serve in offices.

He is to counsel and correct and to preach the gospel to his flock, individually and collectively. In all of this, he is to teach the gospel of Jesus Christ, the Crucifixion, the Atonement, the Resurrection, the Restoration.

I have heard this described as voluntary service because neither the bishop nor his counselors are paid for what they do. They too pay their tithes and offerings, and they devote endless hours to their calling. They are paid only in blessings, as are those who serve with them.

But one does not exactly volunteer or aspire to be bishop. He is *called* to be bishop, "called of God, by prophecy." Then he is both ordained and set apart "by the laying on of hands by those who are in authority, to preach the Gospel and administer in the ordinances thereof" (Articles of Faith 1:5).

A man is *ordained* a bishop, an office in the priesthood; then he is *set apart* and given the keys to preside over a ward. He with his two counselors form a bishopric—a type of presidency.

Once ordained, he is a bishop for the rest of his life. When he is released from presiding over a ward, his ordination becomes dormant. If called again to preside over a ward, his previous ordination is reactivated. When he is released, it becomes dormant again.

Inherent in the ordination to be bishop is both the right and the obligation to be directed by inspiration. The bishop has the power to discern by the Spirit what he is to do.

Revelation is the one credential that all bishops have in common. Bishops come from many cultures, many occupations. They vary in experience, personality, and age, but they do not differ in their right to be guided spiritually.

Years ago a friend of mine went to a large university to study under the ranking authority in the field of counseling and guidance. This professor quickly took an interest in this personable, intelligent young

Latter-day Saint. He attracted attention as he moved through the course work required for a doctor's degree.

He chose the Latter-day Saint bishop as the subject for his dissertation. All went well until he described the ordination of a bishop, the power of discernment, and the right of a bishop to spiritual guidance.

His doctoral committee felt that such references had no place in a scholarly paper, and they insisted that he take them out. He thought he might at least say that Latter-day Saints *believe* the bishop has spiritual insight. But the committee denied him even this, for they would be quite embarrassed to have this spiritual ingredient included in a scholarly dissertation.

He was told that with some little accommodation—specifically, leaving out all the references to revelation—his dissertation would be published and his reputation established.

He did the best he could. His dissertation did not contain enough about the Spirit to satisfy him and too much to be fully accepted by his worldly professors. But he received his degree.

I asked this friend what was the most important thing he had learned in his study of bishops. He answered, "I learned that the mantle is far, far greater than the intellect, that the priesthood is the guiding power."

Do not doubt that an ordinary soul called from the ranks to be bishop can give inspired counsel and correction. Unfortunately, some who could be helped so much are reluctant to seek counsel from the bishop, while others endlessly seem to need counseling and comfort and feel neglected if they are not constantly tended.

Bishops are inspired! Each of us has agency to accept or reject counsel from our leaders, but never disregard the counsel of your bishop, whether given over the pulpit or individually, and never turn down a call from your bishop.

It can be a tough world, a tough life, and in some ways it's even tougher in the Church. Eliza R. Snow wrote:

Think not when you gather to Zion,
Your troubles and trials are through,
That nothing but comfort and pleasure
Are waiting in Zion for you:
No, no, 'tis designed as a furnace,
All substance, all textures to try,
To burn all the "wood . . . and [the] stubble,"
The gold from the dross purify. . . .

Think not when you gather to Zion,
The Saints here have nothing to do
But to look to your personal welfare,
And always be comforting you.
No; those who are faithful are doing
What they find to do with their might;
To gather the scattered of Israel
They labor by day and by night.

(*Hymns* [1948], no. 21)

When we need help, the bishop is there; but be careful not to impose unnecessarily upon his time. Bishops can do only so much. The bishopric must have time to make a living and time for their own families.

Often we are asked how the relatively few Apostles in the First Presidency and the Twelve can manage the Church, now more than ten million strong.

Actually the Church is no bigger than a ward. Each bishop has counselors. He wears a special mantle and is designated as the presiding high priest in the ward. There are other high priests, and there is a presidency of elders. There are auxiliary leaders and teachers sufficient for the need. When we serve obediently, ever willingly, our pay, like the bishop's, comes in blessings.

No matter if the Church grows to be a hundred million (as it surely will!), it will still be no bigger than a ward. Everything needed for our redemption, save for the temple, is centered there—and temples now come ever closer to all of us.

Small numbers of wards are grouped together under the shelter of stakes and branches under districts. There is a stake presidency and a council to train the bishopric and other leaders to train those who serve with them.

This organization, in place across the world, is a product of the restoration of the gospel of Jesus Christ. This miracle of willing service is possible because of individual testimonies of the Redeemer.

The revelation, present when this system was conceived, did not end there, for the purpose of it all is to shelter families. Families are grouped together in a ward or branch.

It is the responsibility of the bishop to see that each family is bound together in enduring covenants and each individual is safe and happy. The system works best when the bishop recognizes the preeminent responsibility of parents.

While the bishop is sometimes referred to as the "father of the ward," we should remember he is not called to rear the children of the ward.

Our handbook states:

"Parents have the first responsibility for the spiritual and physical welfare of their children (see D&C 68:25–28). The bishopric and other . . . leaders support but do not replace parents in this responsibility" (*Handbook 2: Administering the Church* [2010], 51).

"The programs and activities of the Church support and strengthen individuals and families" (*Handbook 2*, 9).

The First Presidency recently wrote to the Church:

"The home is the basis of a righteous life, and no other instrumentality can take its place or fulfill its essential functions in carrying forward this God-given responsibility.

"We counsel parents and children to give highest priority to family prayer, family home evening, gospel study and instruction, and wholesome family activities. However worthy and appropriate other demands or activities may be, they must not be permitted to displace the divinely appointed duties that only parents and families can adequately perform" ("A Letter to Members from the First Presidency," 11 February 1999; see *Church News,* 27 February 1999, 3).

Families, like wards, vary in size and shape. Time moves on; one generation replaces another. Babies are born and mature to become parents and then grandparents. One family divides itself to become several. Wards grow and are divided. Where there was one, there are others.

Whatever happens in the world, whatever heights of civility or depths of depravity emerge in society, the plan remains unaltered. The Church will grow until it fills the whole earth. At once it will remain no bigger than the ward.

The Church provides activities and associations and ordinances and ordinations and covenants and contracts and corrections which prepare each of us for exaltation. It follows a pattern made in the heavens, for no mortal mind could have designed it.

Now and always hereafter, ordinary men will leave their teams standing in an unfinished furrow, the reins draped over the plow, when someone needs help. The women and children serve with them and will sustain them, supplied with truth from the books of revelation, the gem of them all being the Book of Mormon, which testifies of Christ, of the Atonement, of His Resurrection; and I testify of Him.

Sheltered in the ward within the plan which He revealed, we with our families will be safe.

12

TO STAKE PRESIDENTS, SHEPHERDS OF THE FLOCK

I would like to report a conversation I had with a very devoted stake president following a stake conference and a question he asked me to answer.

I was very favorably impressed with the dedication of this faithful man. His stake was well administered; regular meetings were held and were well attended. The programs seemed to be functioning fairly well, and a building program was underway.

But somehow he was troubled. He told of worrisome indicators. Far too many of their young people turned up at the last minute without a desire to serve a mission. And, in spite of all that was done, some were disqualified from serving. Far too many of their youth were diverted from temple marriage.

And some leading families, when viewed as only a bishop or a stake president may view them, were filled with worry and disharmony. And in some, already there was transgression, even divorce.

From an address given at a meeting of Regional Representatives of the Twelve and stake presidents, April 2, 1982.

"We work so hard," he said, "but we don't get the results we deserve for all we do."

And then came the question: "What are we doing wrong?"

That is a good question—a very good question—one, president, that you surely have asked before. I said to him and I say to you: "President, you may not be doing anything that is particularly wrong. You are faithful and dedicated. But there may be some *right* things that you are not doing with enough concentration."

Let me illustrate. In the mountains surrounding the Salt Lake Valley there is very deep snow from November through April. The animals, especially the deer, suffer because of it. They move from the foothills to the orchards and gardens trying to find enough nourishment to survive. President Gordon B. Hinckley, who lived quite near those mountains, had them in his garden during the winter.

For many years, game wardens bought alfalfa hay and established feed yards in the foothills. The deer came in great numbers to eat the green, leafy hay. The wardens thought they were doing all they needed to do for them. But if winter wore on and spring was late, the deer died in great numbers. They died of starvation with their bellies full of hay. This because nutrients essential to sustain life through a long period of stress were missing from their diet.

It can be like that with the flocks for whom we are the shepherds. Other stake presidents have thought they were doing all that was needed for their sheep, only to find that *some had been fed but not nourished.* Like the deer with their stomachs full of hay, in times of prolonged individual stress, members do not survive spiritually.

Buildings and budgets and reports and programs and procedures are very important but by themselves do not carry that essential spiritual nourishment and will not accomplish what the Lord has given us to do. They are only tools—the means to an end, not ends in themselves. These things you ought to do but not leave the very weighty matters undone (see Matthew 23:23).

The *right* things, those with true spiritual nourishment, are centered in the scriptures.

To find the source of sustaining spiritual nourishment and strength, we must go to the revelations. Consider what the Lord has told us:

"We believe in God, the Eternal Father, and in His Son, Jesus Christ, and in the Holy Ghost. . . .

"We believe that through the Atonement of Christ, all mankind may be saved, by obedience to the laws and ordinances of the Gospel. . . .

"We believe that the first principles and ordinances of the Gospel are: first, *Faith* in the Lord Jesus Christ; second, *Repentance;* third, *Baptism* by immersion for the remission of sins; fourth, *Laying on of hands* for the gift of the Holy Ghost" (Articles of Faith 1:1, 3, 4; italics added).

You have been told that the most reliable indicator of spiritual strength in your stake is the number of men who hold the Melchizedek Priesthood. Think what could happen if you were to add to their numbers and increase their worthiness. Few things you do to bless your people will equal in value the attention you give to the quorums of the priesthood. Strengthen the quorums of the priesthood, particularly the higher priesthood.

Ponder this very clear statement from the Doctrine and Covenants:

"This greater priesthood administereth the gospel and holdeth the key of the mysteries of the kingdom, even the key of the knowledge of God.

"Therefore, *in the ordinances* thereof, the power of godliness is manifest.

"And without *the ordinances* thereof, *and the authority of the priesthood,* the power of godliness is not manifest unto men in the flesh" (D&C 84:19–21; italics added).

Brethren, do not forget the priesthood, the ordinances, the covenants, the gospel, the scriptures.

Somehow these things have a tendency to become submerged or

lost in all we have to do. We must not lose sight of them. If we do, we may feed the flock but fail to give them essential spiritual nutrients.

These things slip from our attention partly because they are not listed on our reports. Unfortunately we tend to center our efforts on things that can be written on reports. The most important things we do not and should not and will not require to be put on reports.

We cannot count faith or repentance, nor should we try to compute prayer nor tabulate love. These are spiritual things that do not lend themselves to numbers and percentages.

But even these things can be measured. They lend themselves to spiritual assessment in interviews, through meditation and prayer. They may be appraised by employing the powers of discernment, a precious spiritual gift which accompanies our callings.

Do not become so preoccupied with reports and procedures and programs and buildings that you neglect this part of your ministry.

Ordinance and *covenant* are words that we do not often find on the agendas of stake presidencies, but they should be there. Put them there. Periodically you should consider such questions as these:

- Are all members receiving their ordinances?
- Are they receiving them in proper sequence?
- Is there a conversion for every baptism?
- Is there a pure candidate for every ordination?
- Is there a worthy member for every temple recommend?
- Is the gospel preached in sacrament meetings?
- Is there a true spirit of worship in the meetings?
- Is the gospel taught in plainness in the classes?

Are the quorum presidents sitting in council with their members and teaching them "according to the covenants," as the scriptures require them to do? (D&C 107:89).

These questions, and many like them, should appear on your

agendas from time to time lest you center your time and your attention on things, on reports, that matter less than these things do.

Do not forget discernment, inspiration, admonition, correction, and forgiveness.

Brethren, do not neglect the priesthood, the covenants, the ordinances, the scriptures.

Put them on your agendas; discuss them.

Remember the strongest influence in both conversion and reactivation is the gospel. If the members of your flock do not learn the gospel, they may be fed but not nourished.

Seek for the gift to teach by the Spirit. Then tithing, for instance, becomes less a matter of money than it does of faith and unselfishness and obedience. We then see it as preparation for receiving the ordinances. It becomes a privilege rather than an imposition. We will then teach tithing without hesitation to even the tiniest of children.

If you will heed these things, there will come to you an infusion of spiritual strength and influence that you may not have enjoyed before. Your discernment will deepen; your insights will become more vivid; your capacity to counsel, to teach, to preach, and to administer will be enlarged.

Then when you wrestle with problems of buildings and budgets and programs and procedures and reports, it will be with a purpose. You will know why they are necessary—as a means to an end. And you will know what that end is to be. It is this: Every member should worthily receive the ordinances—baptism, confirmation, the sacrament, administrations, blessings, ordinations, washings, anointings, endowments, sealings—and then they must endure to the end and keep their covenants.

Now we must say a word about your own worthiness. It is not a small thing to be called to preside over a stake of Zion, for you hold "the priesthood . . . after the holiest order of God" (D&C 84:18) or "the Holy Priesthood, after the Order of the Son of God" (D&C 107:3).

You hold sacred authority. Keep your covenants. Be pure and true to your calling.

We are led by a prophet of God, and the ordination of the Apostles as prophets, seers, and revelators is more than just a designation, for with the ordination come the spiritual powers to see and to know.

Before us there are signs of great trials and of great achievements. The enemies encircle about us, angered by our progress. Be ever watchful! For more ominous than this, they are aided by those within who destroy faith and feed that which has no lasting substance.

Do not be discouraged when disappointments come, as surely they will, for every soul has his agency. And some will not follow you, nor will they follow us. That is part of the testing.

Teach your leaders and the parents, particularly the fathers. A worthy father who honors his priesthood, who is faithful to his wife and to his children, can by ordinance have his family sealed to him and become a ruler in a kingdom which shall have no end.

Build the buildings you need, establish the programs, administer your budgets, compile your reports, sponsor your activities—for all these are important tools in the perfecting of the Saints. Use all of them and every other righteous means that you can devise to purify the Church.

Counsel your flock, bless them, teach them, interview them.

If there are the unclean among them, correct them, lead them to the cleansing, healing waters of repentance. Extend the sweet, soothing balm of forgiveness. Dry the tears and ease the pain of those who have stumbled. When they are worthy, ordain them and recommend them to the house of the Lord for their initiatory ordinances, and their endowments, and their sealings.

The Lord will be with you.

13

FUNERALS—
A TIME FOR REVERENCE

A neighbor once told me that as a missionary in earlier days he and his companion were walking along a ridge in the mountains of the South. They saw people gathering in a clearing near a cabin some distance down the hillside. They had come for a funeral. A little boy had drowned, and his parents had sent for the preacher to "say words." The minister, who rode a circuit on horseback, would rarely visit these isolated families. But when there was trouble, they would send for him.

The little fellow was to be buried in a grave opened near the cabin. The elders stayed in the background as the minister stood before the grieving family and began his sermon.

If the parents had hoped for consolation from this man of the cloth, they were disappointed. He scolded them severely because the little boy had not been baptized. He told them bluntly that their little son was lost in endless torment, and it was their fault.

After the grave was covered and the neighbors had gone, the elders

From an address given at general conference, October 1, 1988; see *Ensign*, November 1988, 18–20.

approached the grieving parents. "We are servants of the Lord," they told the sobbing mother, "and we've come with a message for you."

As the grief-stricken parents listened, the elders unfolded the plan of redemption. They quoted from the Book of Mormon, "Little children need no repentance, neither baptism" (Moroni 8:11), and then bore testimony of the restoration of the gospel.

I have sympathy for that itinerant preacher, for he was doing the best he could with the light and knowledge he had. But there is more than he had to give.

What comfort the truth brings at times of sorrow! Since death is ever present with us, a knowledge of how essential it is to the plan of salvation is of immense, practical value. Every one of us should know how and why it came to be in the beginning.

Mortal death came into the world at the Fall.

It is easier for me to understand that word *fall* in the scriptures if I think both in terms of *location* and of *condition*. The word *fall* means to descend to a lower place.

The Fall of man was a move from the presence of God to mortal life on earth. That move down to a lower place came as a consequence of a broken law.

Fall may also describe a change in *condition*. For instance, one can fall in reputation or from prominence. The word *fall* well describes what transpired when Adam and Eve were driven from the garden. A transformation took place in their bodies. The bodies of flesh and bone became temporal bodies. *Temporal* means temporary. The scriptures say, "The life of all flesh is the blood thereof" (Leviticus 17:14; see also Deuteronomy 12:23; *Teachings of the Prophet Joseph Smith,* sel. Joseph Fielding Smith [1976], 199–200, 367).

President Spencer W. Kimball explained, "Blood, the life-giving element in our bodies, replaced the finer substance which coursed through their bodies before. They and we became mortal, subject to illness, pains, and even the physical dissolution called death" ("Absolute Truth," *Ensign,* September 1978, 5).

After the transformation of the Fall, bodies of flesh and bone and *blood* (unlike our spirit bodies) could not endure. Somehow the ingredient of blood carried with it a limit to life. It was as though a clock were set and a time given. Thereafter, all living things moved inexorably toward mortal death.

Temporal, I repeat, means temporary. And so, death is the reality of life. When conditions develop because of age or illness or accident, the spirit is separated from the body.

Death can be tragic with the loss of one upon whom others depend for happiness, for many die too young. Sometimes it is slow in coming to one who yearns to join the loved ones who have gone before. Some sleep peacefully away, while others endure long suffering. And we know that death can be terrible and violent. To threaten or to take life, even our own in suicide, is to offend God, for He "in all things hath forbidden it, from the beginning of man" (Ether 8:19).

It is my conviction that in the spirit world prior to mortal birth, we waited anxiously for our time to enter mortality. I also believe that we were willing to accept whatever conditions would prevail in life. Perhaps we knew that nature might impose limits on the mind or on the body or on life itself. I believe that we nevertheless anxiously awaited our turn.

Funerals

One of the most solemn and sacred meetings of the Church is the funeral for a departed member. It is a time of caring and support when families gather in a spirit of tender regard for one another. It is a time to soberly contemplate doctrines of the gospel and the purposes for the ministry of the Lord Jesus Christ.

Except where burial is prohibited by law, we are counseled to bury our dead. There are important symbolic references to burial in the ordinance of baptism and elsewhere in the doctrines of the Church.

Where required by law, alternate methods of disposing of the remains do not nullify the Resurrection. On occasion a body will be lost through accident or military action. A funeral is nevertheless very important. For we take comfort in the promises in the scriptures of a complete restoration of both the body and the spirit.

A comforting, spiritual funeral is of great importance. It helps console the bereaved and establishes a transition from mourning to the reality that we must move forward with life. Whether death is expected or a sudden shock, an inspirational funeral where the doctrines of resurrection, the mediation of Christ, and the certainty of life after death are taught strengthens those who must now move on with life.

Many attend funerals who do not come to church regularly. They come subdued in spirit and are teachable. How sad when an opportunity for conversion is lost because a funeral is less than it might have been.

Reason to Be Concerned about Funerals

There is reason to fear that we are drifting from the sacred spirit of reverence which should characterize funerals. The Brethren have discussed this in council meetings and are concerned.

I have read what the revelations teach us concerning mortal death, and the instructions given by the Brethren concerning funerals.

May I review some of that counsel. I hope that bishops will pay attention because the responsibility for arranging and conducting funerals in the Church rests upon the bishopric.

Funerals Are Church Meetings

Funerals held under the direction of the priesthood are Church meetings. They have been likened to sacrament meetings. I quote from a priesthood bulletin:

"It is requested that henceforth all funerals conducted under the auspices of the officials of the Church follow the general format of the sacrament meeting with respect to music, speaking, and prayers. Music should be used at the beginning of the service prior to the opening prayer and possibly after the invocation also, as in our Sunday meetings. The closing portion of the funeral likewise should follow our customary pattern of having a final musical number immediately before the concluding prayer. Where feasible, a choir could very well be used on the musical program.

"With respect to speaking, it should be kept in mind that funeral services provide an excellent opportunity for teaching the basic doctrines . . . in a positive manner. . . . Following these suggestions will help to keep our services in line with our established pattern and will avoid practices now so commonly followed elsewhere" (*Priesthood Bulletin,* April 1972).

Bishops, always show tender regard for the family of the deceased, and insofar as their requests accord with established policy, they may willingly be met. On occasion a family member has suggested, sometimes even insisted, that some innovation be added to the funeral service as a special accommodation to the family. Within reason, of course, a bishop may honor such a request. However, there are limits to what may be done without disturbing the spirituality and causing it to be less than it might be. We should remember, too, that others attending the funeral may suppose that innovation is an accepted procedure and introduce it at other funerals. Then, unless we are careful, an innovation which was allowed as an accommodation to one family in one funeral may come to be regarded as expected in every funeral.

Occasionally a mortician, out of a desire to be of help and not understanding the doctrines and procedures of the Church, will alter a funeral service. Bishops should remember that when funerals are held under priesthood auspices, the service should conform to the instructions given by the Church. We should regard the bishop rather than the family or the mortician as the presiding authority in these matters.

In recent years, there has been a tendency to stray from the accepted pattern for funerals. Sometimes the casket is kept open during the funeral, and members are expected to file by at the close of the funeral. And, instead of the simple family prayer, talks, even musical numbers, have been added at the closing of the casket or at the cemetery before the grave is dedicated. I do not refer to graveside services which may on occasion take the place of a formal funeral. I refer to those alterations of the approved simple agenda for funerals.

When innovations are suggested by family members, morticians, or others, which are quite out of harmony with that agenda, the bishop should quietly persuade them to follow the established pattern. It is not a rigid pattern and allows sufficient flexibility to have each funeral personally appropriate for the deceased.

Family Speaker

There now seems to be the expectation that members of the immediate family must speak at funerals. While that may not be out of order, it should not be regarded as required. Family members ordinarily give the family prayer and dedicate the grave.

If family members do speak, and I repeat, it is not a requirement, they are under the same obligation to speak with reverence and to teach the principles of the gospel.

Sometimes family members tell things that would be appropriate at a family reunion or at some other family gathering but not on an occasion that should be sacred and solemn. While quiet humor is not out of order in a funeral, it should be wisely introduced. It should be ever kept in mind that the funeral should be characterized by spirituality and reverence.

One statement from the instructions refers to events other than the funeral service itself. I quote: "The bishop urges members to maintain a spirit of reverence, dignity, and solemnity during a funeral service and at gatherings connected with the service" (*Handbook 2: Administering the Church* [2010], 147).

That should be kept in mind if a viewing is to be held. Viewings are not mandatory.

Funerals generally bring relatives and friends from distant places. There is the tendency to greet one another joyfully and, unfortunately, at times noisily. Some visit at length, showing little regard for others who are waiting to pay their respects. Both the irreverence and the delay are discourtesies from which the spirituality of the occasion suffers.

Renewing of friendships should appropriately be made outside the room where the viewing is taking place. Local leaders need to caution us gently on this matter. Surely we do not want to be known as an irreverent people.

There is the need to reestablish the spirit of reverence at funerals, whether in a chapel, a mortuary, or at other locations.

We should always have a tender regard for the feelings of the bereaved.

We are close, very close, to the spirit world at the time of death. There are tender feelings, spiritual communications really, which may easily be lost if there is not a spirit of reverence.

At times of sorrow and parting, one may experience that "peace . . . which passeth all understanding" (Philippians 4:7) which the scriptures promise. That is a very private experience. Many have come to marvel in their hearts that such a feeling of peace, even exaltation, can come at the time of such grief and uncertainty.

Testimonies are strengthened by such inspiration, and we come to know, personally know, what is meant when the Lord said, "I will not leave you comfortless: I will come to you" (John 14:18).

The Comforter works, as far as I have experience, in moments of reverence and quiet and solemnity. How sad if our own conduct is irreverent at a time when others are seeking so desperately for spiritual strength.

The revelations tell us that "thou shalt live together in love, insomuch that thou shalt weep for the loss of them that die, and more especially for those that have not hope of a glorious resurrection" (D&C 42:45).

A funeral may be a happy-sad occasion when death comes as a welcome release. Nevertheless, it is a sacred occasion and should be characterized by solemnity and reverence.

Alma's son thought that death was unfair. In his remarkable sermon on repentance, Alma taught his son about death, saying, "Now behold, it was not expedient that man should be reclaimed from this temporal death, for that would destroy the great plan of happiness" (Alma 42:8).

Alma did not say that setting mortal death aside would merely delay or disturb the plan of happiness; he said it would *destroy* it.

The words *death* and *happiness* are not close companions in mortality, but in the eternal sense they are essential to one another. Death is a mechanism of rescue. Our first parents left Eden. The mortal death they brought upon themselves, and upon us, is our journey home.

Three elements combine in a funeral as in no other meeting: the doctrines of the gospel, the spirit of inspiration, and families gathered in tender regard for one another.

May we reintroduce the attitude of reverence each time we gather to memorialize one who has moved through the veil to that place where one day each of us will go.

No consolation in parting compares with that "peace . . . which passeth all understanding." That is fostered by reverence. Reverence, please, Brothers and Sisters, reverence.

PART FOUR

YOUTH AND FAMILY

14

"YE ARE THE TEMPLE OF GOD"

I respond to a prompting I have had for a very long time to address the youth of the Church who face challenges unknown to us in our youth.

President J. Reuben Clark described our youth as "hungry for things of the spirit; they are eager to learn the Gospel, and they want it straight, undiluted.

"They want to know about . . . our beliefs; they want to gain testimonies of their truth; they are not now doubters but inquirers, seekers after truth. . . .

"You do not have to sneak up behind this spiritually experienced youth and whisper religion in [their] ears; you can come right out, face to face, and talk with [them]. . . . You can bring these truths to [them] openly. . . . Youth may prove to be not more fearful of them than you are. There is no need for gradual approaches" ("The Charted Course of the Church in Education," in Boyd K. Packer, *Teach Ye Diligently*, rev. ed. [1991], 365, 373–74).

From an address given at general conference, October 8, 2000; see *Ensign*, November 2000, 72–74.

I agree with President Clark and will speak plainly to the youth about things I have learned and know to be true.

When I was eighteen, I was called into military service. I had not received my patriarchal blessing, so the bishop recommended me to a patriarch near the air base.

Patriarch J. Roland Sandstrom of the Santa Ana California Stake gave me my blessing. In it I was told this: "You made a free and willing decision to abide by the laws of Eternal Progress as outlined by our elder brother, the Lord Jesus Christ. You . . . have been . . . given a physical body with which you might experience Earth Life, . . . a body of such physical proportions and fitness as to enable your spirit to function through it unhampered by physical impediments. . . . Cherish this as a great heritage" (patriarchal blessing of Boyd K. Packer, 15 January 1944, 1).

That was a great comfort to me. Because of childhood polio, I was not able to participate in sports and was left with a feeling of inferiority when compared to my friends.

My patriarchal blessing further counseled: "Guard and protect [your body]—take nothing into it that shall harm the organs thereof because it is sacred. It is the instrument of your mind and the foundation of your character."

I found in the Word of Wisdom a principle with a promise. The principle: Care for your body; avoid habit-forming stimulants, tea, coffee, tobacco, liquor, and drugs (see D&C 89:3–9). Such addictive things do little more than relieve a craving which they caused in the first place.

The promise: Those who obey will receive better health (see D&C 89:18) and "great treasures of knowledge, even hidden treasures" (D&C 89:19).

The Prophet Joseph Smith said: "We came to this earth that we might have a body and present it pure before God in the celestial kingdom. The great principle of happiness consists in having a body. The devil has no body, and herein is his punishment. He is pleased when he can obtain the tabernacle of man. . . . All beings who have bodies have power over those who have not" (*Teachings of the Prophet Joseph Smith,* sel. Joseph Fielding Smith [1976], 181).

Even the severe tests of health or a handicapped or disabled body can refine a soul for the glorious day of restoration and healing which surely will come.

Your body really *is* the instrument of your mind and the foundation of your character.

President Harold B. Lee taught of the important symbolic and actual effect of how we dress and groom our bodies. If you are well groomed and modestly dressed, you invite the companionship of the Spirit of our Father in Heaven and exercise a wholesome influence upon those around you. To be unkempt in your appearance exposes you to influences that are degrading (see *The Teachings of Harold B. Lee,* ed. Clyde J. Williams [1996], 220).

Avoid immodest clothing. Dress and groom to show the Lord that you know how precious your body is.

President Gordon B. Hinckley warned you not to decorate your body with pictures or symbols that will never wash off or to pierce your body with rings or jewelry after the manner of the world (see "Your Greatest Challenge, Mother," *Ensign,* November 2000, 97).

You would not paint a temple with dark pictures or symbols or graffiti or even initials. Do not do so with your body.

"Know ye not that your body is the temple of the Holy Ghost which is in you, which ye have of God, and ye are not your own?

"For ye are bought with a price: therefore glorify God in your body, and in your spirit, which are God's" (1 Corinthians 6:19–20).

"Know ye not that ye are the temple of God, and that the Spirit of God dwelleth in you?

"If any man defile the temple of God, him shall God destroy; for the temple of God is holy, which temple ye are" (1 Corinthians 3:16–17).

There is in your body the supernal power to create life. Boys grow up to be men and may become fathers; girls grow up to be women and may become mothers. Natural and good feelings draw men and women together.

"All human beings—male and female—are created in the image of God. Each is a beloved spirit son or daughter of heavenly parents, and, as such, each has a divine nature and destiny. Gender is an essential characteristic of individual premortal, mortal, and eternal identity and purpose" ("The Family: A Proclamation to the World," *Ensign*, November 1995, 102).

"Marriage between a man and a woman is ordained of God and . . . the family is central to the Creator's plan for the eternal destiny of His children" ("The Family," 102).

You should be attracted to one another and to marry. Then, and only then, may you worthily respond to the strong and good and constant desire to express that love through which children will bless your lives. By commandment of God our Father, that must happen only between husband and wife—man and woman—committed to one another in the covenant of marriage (see 1 Corinthians 7:2; D&C 42:22). To do otherwise is forbidden and will bring sorrow.

It is about controlling these natural desires that the strictest commandments are given in the revelations (see Smith, *Teachings,* 181; Galatians 5:19; Ephesians 5:5; Mormon 9:28).

Young men and women, keep yourselves worthy. Stay away from those environments, the music, the films, the videos, the clubs, and the associations that draw you into immoral conduct (see 1 Corinthians 6:9; 1 Thessalonians 5:22; 2 Timothy 2:22; D&C 9:13).

Now, I turn to another danger, almost unknown in years past but now everywhere about you.

Normal desires and attractions emerge in the teenage years; there is the temptation to experiment, to tamper with the sacred power of procreation. These desires can be intensified, even perverted, by pornography, improper music, or the encouragement from unworthy associations. What would have been only a more or less normal passing phase in establishing gender identity can become implanted and leave you confused, even disturbed.

If you consent, the adversary can take control of your thoughts and lead you carefully toward a habit and to an addiction, convincing you that immoral, unnatural behavior is a fixed part of your nature.

With some few, there is the temptation which seems nearly over-powering for man to be attracted to man or woman to woman. The scriptures plainly condemn those who "dishonour their own bodies between themselves; . . . men with men working that which is unseemly" (Romans 1:24, 27) or "women [who] change the natural use into that which is against nature" (Romans 1:26).

The gates of freedom, and the good or bad beyond, swing open or closed to the password *choice*. You are free to choose a path that may lead to despair, to disease, even to death (see 2 Nephi 2:26–27).

If you choose that course, the fountains of life may dry up. You will not experience the combination of love and struggle, the pain and pleasure, the disappointment and sacrifice, that love which, blended together in parenthood, exalts a man or a woman and leads to that fulness of joy spoken of in the scriptures (see 2 Nephi 2:25; 9:18; D&C 11:13; 42:61; 101:36).

Do not experiment; do not let anyone of either gender touch your body to awaken passions that can flame beyond control. It begins as an innocent curiosity, Satan influences your thoughts, and it becomes a pattern, a habit, which may imprison you in an addiction, to the sorrow and disappointment of those who love you (see John 8:34; 2 Peter 2:12–14, 18–19).

Pressure is put upon legislatures to legalize unnatural conduct. They can never make right that which is forbidden in the laws of God (see Leviticus 18:22; 1 Corinthians 6:9; 1 Timothy 1:9–10).

Sometimes we are asked why we do not recognize this conduct

as a diverse and acceptable lifestyle. This we cannot do. We did not make the laws; they were made in heaven "before the foundation of the world" (D&C 132:5; 124:41; see also Alma 22:13). We are servants only.

Just as with the prophets in ancient times, we have been "conse-crated priests and teachers of this people, . . . [responsible to] magnify our office unto the Lord, taking upon us the responsibility, answering the sins of the people upon our own heads if we did not teach them the word of God with all diligence" (Jacob 1:18–19).

We understand why some feel we reject them. That is not true. We *do not* reject them, only their immoral behavior. We *cannot* reject them, for they are the sons and daughters of God. We *will not* reject them, because we love them (see Hebrews 12:6–9; Romans 3:19; Helaman 15:3; D&C 95:1).

These people may even feel that we do not love them. That also is not true. Parents know, and one day they will know, that there are times when parents and we who lead the Church must extend *tough* love because failing to teach and to warn and to discipline is to destroy.

We did not make the rules; they were revealed as commandments. We do not cause nor can we prevent the consequences if one disobeys the moral laws (see D&C 101:78). In spite of criticism or opposition, we must teach and we must warn.

When any unworthy desires press into your own mind, fight them, resist them, control them (see James 4:6–8; 2 Nephi 9:39; Mosiah 3:19). The Apostle Paul taught, "There hath no temptation taken you but such as is common to man: but God is faithful, who will not suffer you to be tempted above that ye are able; but will with the temptation also make a way to escape, that ye may be able to bear it" (1 Corinthians 10:13; see also D&C 62:1).

That may be a struggle from which some will not be free in this life. But if you do not act on temptations, you need feel no guilt. They may be extremely difficult to resist. But that is better than to yield and bring disappointment and unhappiness to you and those who love you.

Some think that God created them with overpowering, unnatural desires, that they are trapped and not responsible (see James 1:13–15). That is not true. It cannot be true. Even if they were to accept it as true, they must remember that He can cure and He can heal (see Alma 7:10–13; 15:8).

Now, what of those who have already made mistakes or have lost themselves to an immoral lifestyle? What hope do they have? Are they cast off and lost forever?

These are not unforgivable sins. However unworthy or unnatural or immoral these transgressions may be, they are not unforgivable (see D&C 42:25). When they are completely forsaken and fully repented of, there can open the purifying gift of forgiveness, and the burden of guilt will be erased. There is a way back—long, perhaps; hard, certainly; possible, of course! (see Acts 5:31; Ephesians 1:7; Mosiah 4:2; 26:29; D&C 1:31–32; 58:42; 61:2).

You need not, you cannot, find your way alone. You have a Redeemer. The Lord will lift your burden if you choose to repent and turn from your sins and do them no more. That is what the Atonement of Christ was for.

"Come now, and let us reason together, saith the Lord: though your sins be as scarlet, they shall be as white as snow; though they be red like crimson, they shall be as wool" (Isaiah 1:18).

The choice rests with you; you are not cast off forever. I repeat, these transgressions are not unforgivable.

One may think, *It is too late, my life will soon be over, and I am eternally doomed.* Not so, for "if in this life only we have hope in Christ, we are of all men most miserable" (1 Corinthians 15:19).

Just as the physical body can be cleansed and healed, so can the spirit be washed clean by the power of the Atonement. The Lord will lift you and carry your burden during the suffering and struggle required to make you clean. That is what the Atonement of Christ is all about. He said, "I, the Lord, [will] remember [your sins] no more" (D&C 58:42; see also Hebrews 8:12; 10:17; Alma 36:19).

Our beloved, precious youth, stay in the Lord's way. If you stumble, rise up, go on. If you have lost your way, we open our arms and await your return.

God be praised for the cleansing, purifying, forgiving power of the Atonement brought by the Lord Jesus Christ, of whom I bear witness.

15

THE OTHER SIDE
OF THE SHIP

Some time ago, two unusual gatherings of young people caught the attention of the world. At White Lake, New York, nearly half a million young people gathered.

Later a similar gathering was held on the Isle of Wight. They came from all countries, from all levels of society.

These meetings were billed as music festivals. Certainly they did not come to hear the music—they came to be there.

Such gatherings, so appealing to our youth, are unique in history, and they mean something.

Some suppose that the youth responded to political or philosophical motivation. It is not so. It would be a mistake to so conclude, even though some youth are indeed deeply entangled in the political and social issues of today.

From an address given at general conference, October 3, 1969; see *Improvement Era*, December 1969, 57–59.

Unquenched Spiritual Desire

Many youth frantically cling to whatever social issue is foremost at the moment, not realizing perhaps that it is not so much the cause that ignites them; rather, it is having a cause that satisfies their need. Neither is it an intellectual movement, although it has many of the attributes. Nor is it a cultural one, though they have developed their own style of music, vocabulary, art forms, and poetry. It is spiritual motivation that brings these young people together.

They may not know it, but a whole generation of youth is athirst with an unquenched spiritual desire. As has been foretold:

"Behold, the days come, saith the Lord God, that I will send a famine in the land, not a famine of bread, nor a thirst for water, but of hearing the words of the Lord:

"And they shall wander from sea to sea, and from the north even to the east, they shall run to and fro to seek the word of the Lord, and shall not find it.

"In that day shall the fair virgins and young men faint for thirst" (Amos 8:11–13).

Thirst for Life's Meaning

Youth suffer from a lingering thirst that has become a drive. Though it gnaws within them, it is not physical. They want to know what it all means—they are seeking the true meaning of life. There is something missing from their lives, some vital substance that they have not tasted.

Many of them unfortunately seek it in physical satisfaction. They smash down the boundaries of morality and wantonly indulge themselves in every manner conceivable to the limit of physical experience, seeking in physical gratification some taste of life. They come away less satisfied than before, the thirst and the craving more acute.

Escape from Futility

Then many of them turn elsewhere, seeking to escape the futility in life. They turn to drugs and find for a moment the escape they seek. At last their spirits soar. They reach beyond themselves, erase all limitations, and taste for a moment, as they suppose, that which they have been seeking. But it is a synthetic, a wicked counterfeit, for they return to a depression worse than the one they left.

Then they become players in the saddest of human tragedies. For, as they turn again to this release, they are not seeking what they sought before but indulge to escape the consequences of each previous adventure with drugs. This is addiction! This is tragedy! This is slavery! When a remedy becomes worse than the disease, then we have found futility itself.

Advice to Young People

If one of these young people would listen for a moment—listen seriously enough that I could speak from the depths of my soul—there are some things I would tell him.

Why, he may first ask, do you appeal to me, the most criticized and uncomfortable of all in society? That is easy to answer.

First, you are right, you know, when you assess that most of society is interested only in immediate material success, too comfortable to really care, too preoccupied to listen to any significant message.

Because you are trying to change things, perhaps you will at least listen.

We are trying to change things too. We have many thousands of young people, something like yourself, who are missionaries assigned across the world to change people. But they must sift through literally thousands to find one who will listen—really listen.

We appeal to you because you are young. Our message requires a change so monumental that few but youth have the courage for it.

Cast the Net on the Right Side

In your rebellion, so called, you have cut yourself loose from your moorings, perhaps even from family ties, and are set adrift on the sea of life. Now you may be drifting on the right sea—you may even be in the right boat—but you might try fishing on the other side. Some others were fishing on the wrong side of the ship.

"And he said unto them, Cast the net on the right side of the ship, and ye shall find. They cast therefore, and now they were not able to draw it for the multitude of fishes" (John 21:6).

When we mention that there is a spiritual answer to your need, I hope you don't dismiss it or ridicule the possibility. If you haven't tried it yet, you are as yet no witness on the matter. Surely you have that much honesty.

You may say you've been to church, that you've tried religion and have not been satisfied. That is little wonder. It isn't in them all, you know, only a flavoring of it. The substance of it, the fullness of it can be found in only one place. Perhaps you have looked for it here, in that one place, and have not found it. And so I repeat, you might try fishing on the right side.

Finding the True Light

No one can compel you to taste of this living water. It can come only when you consent. There are no conscripts, only volunteers.

If you are to find it, you must pay more, by a thousandfold, than ever you paid before, reach farther than you have ever reached, use more courage and self-discipline than you ever knew you had. But at the end of all that comes the promise:

"Verily, thus saith the Lord: It shall come to pass that every soul who forsaketh his sins and cometh unto me, and calleth on my name, and obeyeth my voice, and keepeth my commandments, shall see my face and know that I am;

"And that I am the true light that lighteth every man that cometh into the world" (D&C 93:1–2).

I must be plain also to say to you, my young friend, that when you come to know, it will be on His terms—not on yours.

"Therefore," He has said, "sanctify yourselves that your minds become single to God, and the days will come that you shall see him; for he will unveil his face unto you, and it shall be *in his own time, and in his own way, and according to his own will*" (D&C 88:68; italics added).

Facing Issues with New Light

The fact—the positive, irrefutable truth—is that what you seek, my young friend, exists. And when you find it, it will not take you out of the world. You will find a greater need to be in the mainstream of life facing the same issues that are so disturbing to you now, but you'll face them with a different light.

It will not require that you give up anything essential or fulfilling in life, whether it be physical, emotional, spiritual, or intellectual. You will be the same height, the same weight; you'll be under the necessity of eating to live and being sheltered. You'll have dislikes and likes, passions and desires. At first glance nothing will change at all, and yet positively everything will change.

Quench Spiritual Thirst

We bid you—our restless, drifting, seeking youth—to come, quench that spiritual thirst.

The Lord has said: "Whosoever drinketh of . . . water shall thirst again:

"But whosoever drinketh of the water that I shall give him shall never thirst; but the water that I shall give him shall be in him a well of water springing up into everlasting life" (John 4:13–14).

Oh, how we pray that as you drift, seeking everywhere, trying everything, that one day you will cast your net on the right side of the ship.

I bear to you my witness, as one among those authorized to bear that witness, that God does live, Jesus is the Christ, this is his church, The Church of Jesus Christ of Latter-day Saints. He directs His church and ministers in the midst of His Saints. There is a prophet of God directing this work. Youth is needed to carry it on. We bid you to come.

16

"CHILDREN ARE AN HERITAGE OF THE LORD"

Some years ago two of our little boys were wrestling on the rug before the fireplace. They had reached the pitch—you know the one—where laughter turns to tears and play becomes a struggle. I worked a foot gently between them and lifted the older boy (then just four years of age) to a sitting position on the rug, saying, "Hey there, you monkey, you had better settle down." He folded his little arms and looked at me with surprising seriousness. His little boy feelings had been hurt, and he protested, "I not a monkey, Daddy—I a person."

I thought how deeply I loved him, how much I wanted him to be "a person"—one of eternal worth. For "children are an heritage of the Lord" (Psalm 127:3).

That lesson has lingered with me. Among the many things we have learned from our children, this, perhaps, has been the most tempering.

Much of what I know—of what it matters that one knows—I have learned from my children.

From an address given at general conference, October 2, 1966; see *Improvement Era*, December 1966, 1149–50; or Conference Report, October 1966, 131–33.

Parenthood is the greatest of educational experiences. Our children and the children and youth in the Church are great teachers. Let me illustrate with two lessons.

In the days of the pioneer settlements, it was not uncommon to have a ward marshal whose assignment it was, under the direction of the bishop, to maintain orderly conduct among the teenagers.

On a Sunday evening after sacrament meeting, the ward marshal at the little settlement of Corinne came upon a buggy with some teenagers. Since it was his responsibility to check on the young people, he stealthily crept near the buggy to see just what was going on. He managed to reach a rather insufficient tree very close to the buggy just as the moon came out. He had to stand more or less at attention to keep from being seen, but he could easily hear all that was transpiring in the buggy.

Later, in reporting it to the bishop, he told of what had gone on. There had been some jokes told, much laughter, and the usual teenage chatter. He said they sang several songs. The bishop interrupted his report with the question, "Well, was there anything out of order in that situation?" His answer, "Yes! me behind that blamed tree."

Always our youth are teaching those of us who are older, and they teach serious, sacred lessons, too.

"When Do I Die?"

President Joseph T. Bentley presided over the Mexican Mission. I recall hearing him tell an incident that happened, I think, somewhere in Mexico. An eleven-year-old boy had been seriously injured in an automobile accident. By the time they got him to the doctor, he was dying from loss of blood. In looking for a donor for an emergency transfusion, the doctor decided on the boy's seven-year-old sister. He explained to the little girl that her brother was dying and asked whether she would be willing to donate her blood in order to save his life. The little girl turned pale with fright, but in a moment she consented to do it.

The transfusion was made, and the doctor came to the little girl. "The color is coming back into his face," he said. "It looks as though he is going to be all right." She was happy her brother would be all right but said, "But doctor, when am I going to die?" She had thought all the time that she was not just giving her blood but literally her life to save an older brother. We learn great lessons from our youth.

With parenthood such a glorious experience, how important it is that we have reverence for it.

Frequently I receive letters and not infrequently young couples come, particularly of college age, struggling to achieve advanced degrees, and they ask for counsel on the coming of children in their lives.

Planned Parenthood

Never has a generation been so surrounded with those who speak irreverently of life. Never has there been such persuasion to avoid responsibilities of parenthood. Never has it been so convenient to block that frail footpath of life across which new spirits enter mortality.

Several years ago, while representing the Church at the University of Montana, I found myself on a panel with representatives from several churches. The moderator asked each of us to respond to the question, "Do you believe in planned parenthood?" My answer was a resounding "yes!" with this explanation: We plan to have families.

Often when young couples come, they ask the specific question, "How many children should we plan to have?" This I cannot answer, for it is not within my province to know. With some persons there are no restrictions of health, and perhaps a number of children will be born into the family. Some good parents who would have large families are blessed with but one or two children.

And, occasionally, couples who make wonderful parents are not able to have natural offspring and enjoy the marvelous experience of fostering children born to others. Planned parenthood involves a good deal more than just the begetting of children. Nothing in our lives deserves more planning than our responsibilities in parenthood.

I am concerned because our young couples are often in a quandary, particularly when the arbitrary limiting of families is represented as an act of social good.

Young couples are continually told that parenthood means forfeiture of advanced degrees and limiting of occupational progress, a representation they will live to know is false.

Approach Parenthood with Reverence

Whether you will be blessed with many children or but a few, or perhaps experience parenthood through the raising of little ones left homeless, is a matter that will be made known as your life unfolds. But I urge you, I warn you to approach parenthood with reverence. When you covenant in marriage and are free to act in the creation of life, when you stand at the threshold of parenthood, know that you stand on holy ground. Recognize also that in those areas of greatest opportunity lie the snares of persistent temptation.

We are grateful for our family, grateful for all of our children. We have learned so much from them, some of the things we weren't conscious that we wanted to know. Each of them is needed and wanted in our family; and again, much of what I know, of that which matters that one knows, I have learned from our children.

Young couples, draw reverently close to your Father in Heaven in these monumental decisions of life. Seek inspiration from the teachings of the gospel of Jesus Christ. Grow close to Him. Perhaps you, as He, will come to "suffer the little children to come unto [you], and forbid them not: for of such is the kingdom of God" (Mark 10:14).

17

PARENTS IN ZION

I have served in the Quorum of the Twelve Apostles for twenty-eight years and nine years as an Assistant to the Twelve. Put together, that makes thirty-seven years—exactly half my life.

But I have another calling which I have held even longer. I am a parent—a father and a grandfather. It took years to earn the *grandfather* title—another twenty years the title of *great-grandfather*. These titles—*father, grandfather, mother, grandmother*—carry responsibility and an authority which comes in part from experience. Experience is a compelling teacher.

My calling in the priesthood defines my position in the Church; the title *grandfather*, my position in the family. I want to look at both positions together.

Parenthood stands among the most important activities to which Latter-day Saints may devote themselves. Many members face conflicts

From an address given at general conference, October 3, 1998; see *Ensign*, November 1998, 22–24.

as they struggle to balance their responsibilities as parents with faithful activity in the Church.

There are things vital to the well-being of a family which can be found only by going to church. There is the priesthood, which empowers a man to lead and bless his wife and children, and covenants which bind them together forever.

The Church was commanded to "meet together often" (D&C 20:55) and told "when ye are assembled together ye shall instruct and edify each other" (D&C 43:8). Mosiah and Alma gave the same instruction to their people (see Mosiah 18:25; Alma 6:6).

We are commanded to "turn the heart[s] of the fathers to the children, and the heart[s] of the children to their fathers" (Malachi 4:6; see also 3 Nephi 25:5–6; D&C 2:2–3).

The Lord addressed Joseph Smith Jr. by name and said, "You have not kept the commandments, and must needs stand rebuked" (D&C 93:47). He had failed to teach his children. That is the only time the word *rebuke* is used in correcting him.

His counselor Frederick G. Williams was under the same condemnation: "You have not taught your children light and truth" (see D&C 93:41–42). Sidney Rigdon was told the same thing, as was Bishop Newel K. Whitney (D&C 93:44, 50), and the Lord added, "What I say unto one I say unto all" (D&C 93:49).

We have watched the standards of morality sink ever lower until now they are in a free fall. At the same time we have seen an outpouring of inspired guidance for parents and for families.

The whole of curriculum and all activities of the Church have been restructured and correlated with the home:

- Ward teaching became home teaching.
- Family home evening was reestablished.
- Genealogy was renamed family history and set to collect records of all the families.

- And then the historic proclamation on the family was issued by the First Presidency and the Council of the Twelve Apostles.
- The family became, and remains, a prevailing theme in meetings, conferences, and councils.
- All as a prelude to an era of building temples wherein the authority to seal families together forever is exercised.

Can you see the spirit of inspiration resting upon the servants of the Lord and upon parents? Can we withstand the challenge and the assault that is now leveled at the family?

In providing out-of-home activities for the family, we must use care; otherwise, we could be like a father determined to provide everything for his family. He devotes every energy to that end and succeeds; only then does he discover that what they needed most, to be together as a family, has been neglected. And he reaps sorrow in place of contentment.

How easy it is, in our desire to provide schedules of programs and activities, to overlook the responsibilities of the parent and the essential need for families to have time together.

We must be careful lest programs and activities of the Church become too heavy for some families to carry. The principles of the gospel, where understood and applied, strengthen and protect both individuals and families. Devotion to the family and devotion to the Church are not different and separate things.

I recently saw a woman respond when it was said of another, "Since she had the new baby, she isn't doing anything in the Church." You could almost see a baby in the woman's arms as she protested with emotion: "She *is* doing something in the Church. She gave that baby life. She nurtures and teaches it. She is doing the most important thing that she can do in the Church."

How would you respond to this question: "Because of their handicapped child, she is confined to the home and he works two jobs to meet the extra expenses. They seldom attend—can we count them as active in the Church?"

And have you ever heard a woman say, "My husband is a very good father, but he's never been a bishop or a stake president or done anything important in the Church." In response to that, a father vigorously said, "What is more important in the Church than being a good father?"

Every call, every service in the Church brings experience and valuable insights which carry over into family life. Faithful attendance at church, together with careful attention to the needs of the family, is a near-perfect combination. In Church we are taught the great plan of happiness (see Alma 12:32). At home we apply what we have learned.

Would our perspective be more clear if we could, for a moment, look upon parenthood as a calling in the Church? Actually, it is so much more than that; but if we could look at it that way for a moment, we could reach a better balance in the way we schedule families.

I do not want anyone to use what follows as an excuse for turning down an inspired call from the Lord. I *do* want to encourage leaders to carefully consider the home lest they issue calls or schedule activities which place an unnecessary burden on parents and families.

Recently I read a letter from a young couple whose callings in the Church frequently require them to hire a sitter for their small children in order for them to attend their meetings. It has become very difficult for both of them to be home with their children at the same time. Can you see something out of balance there?

Every time you schedule a youngster, you schedule a family—particularly the mother.

Consider the mother who, in addition to her own Church calling and that of her husband, must get her children ready and run from one activity to another. Some mothers become discouraged—even depressed. I receive letters using the word *guilt* because they cannot do it all.

Attending church is, or should be, a respite from the pressures of everyday life. It should bring peace and contentment. If it brings pressure and discouragement, then something is out of balance.

And the Church is not the only responsibility parents have. Other agencies have a very legitimate reason to call upon the resources of the family—schools, employers, community—all need to be balanced in.

Recently a mother told me her family had moved from a rural, scattered ward where, of necessity, activities were consolidated into one weekday night. It was wonderful. They had time for their family. I can see them sitting around the table together.

They moved west into a larger ward where members were closer to the chapel. She said, "Now our family is scheduled Tuesday night, Wednesday night, Thursday night, Friday night, Saturday night, and Sunday night. It is very hard on our family."

Remember, when you schedule a youngster, you schedule a family—particularly the mother.

Most families try very hard; but some, when burdened with problems of health and finance, simply become exhausted trying to keep up, and eventually they withdraw into inactivity. They do not see that they are moving from the one best source of light and truth, of help with their family, into the shadows where danger and heartbreak await.

I must touch upon what must surely be the most difficult problem to solve. Some youngsters receive very little teaching and support at home. There is no question but that we must provide for them. But if we provide a constant schedule of activities sufficient to compensate for the loss in those homes, it may make it difficult for attentive parents to have time to be with and teach their own children. Only prayer and inspiration can lead us to find this difficult balance.

We often hear, "We must provide frequent and exciting activities lest our youth go to less wholesome places." Some of them will. But I have the conviction that if we teach parents to be responsible and allow them sufficient time, over the long course their children will be at home.

There, at home, they can learn what cannot be effectively taught in either church or school. At home they can learn to work and to take responsibility. They can learn what to do when they have children of their own.

For example, in the Church children are taught the principle of tithing, but it is at home that the principle is applied. At home even young children can be shown how to figure a tithe and how it is paid.

One time President and Sister Harold B. Lee were in our home. Sister Lee put a handful of pennies on a table before our young son. She had him slide the shiny ones to one side and said, "These are your tithing; these belong to the Lord. The others are yours to keep." He thoughtfully looked from one pile to the other and then said, "Don't you have any more dirty ones?" That was when the real teaching moment began!

The ward council is the perfect place to establish the balance between home and Church. Here the brethren of the priesthood, themselves fathers, and sisters of the auxiliaries, themselves mothers, can, with inspired insight, coordinate the work of the organizations, each of which serves different members of the family.

Members of the council can compare what each organization is providing for each member and how much time and money is required. They can unite rather than divide families and provide watchful care over single parents, the childless, the unmarried, the elderly, the handicapped—and provide much more than just activities for the children and young people.

The ward council has resources often overlooked. For instance, grandparents, while not filling callings, can help young families who are finding their way along the same path they once walked.

The Lord warned parents, "Inasmuch as parents have children in Zion, . . . that teach them not to understand the doctrine of repentance, faith in Christ the Son of the living God, and of baptism and the gift of the Holy Ghost by the laying on of the hands, when eight years old, the sin be upon the heads of the parents" (D&C 68:25).

The ward council is ideal for our present need. Here the home and the family can be anchored in place, and the Church can support rather than supplant the parents. Fathers and mothers will understand both their obligation to teach their children and the blessings provided by the Church.

As the world grows ever more threatening, the powers of heaven draw ever closer to families and parents.

I have studied much in the scriptures and have taught from them. I have read much from what the prophets and apostles have spoken. They have had a profound influence upon me as a man and as a father.

But most of what I know about how our Father in Heaven really feels about us, His children, I have learned from the way I feel about my wife and my children and their children. This I have learned at home. I have learned it from my parents and from my wife's parents, from my beloved wife and from my children and therefore can testify of a loving Heavenly Father and of a redeeming Lord.

18

MOTHERS

There has lingered in my mind a sentence from the inspired voice of President David O. McKay. "Pure hearts," he said, "in a pure home are always in whispering distance of heaven" (Conference Report, April 1964, 5). This touched my heart. From it, and from the whispered prayer of a little youngster, I take assurance and find an unexpected preface for the subject "Suffer the little children to come unto me" (Mark 10:14).

An associate of mine had a little girl undergo surgery. They arranged for one of the parents to stay with the little youngster during the period of recuperation—for a hospital can be a strange and a frightening place for a little youngster who is injured or ill.

Coincidentally she shared a room at the hospital with another little girl just the same age who had also undergone surgery. During the long, painful hours following the operation, this little girl struggled almost convulsively against the pain, pleading incessantly for her parents.

From an address given at general conference, April 5, 1964; see *Improvement Era*, June 1964, 491–92; or Conference Report, April 1964, 84–86.

"Mister," she would beg, "will you please go find my mommy?" My friend, and in turn his wife, found themselves more at the bed of this little girl than of their own child, for she seemed to need them more.

Finally in the evening hours her parents appeared. They hurriedly visited for a few minutes in a casual way and then nervously observed that they had a social engagement and left the little youngster to face her agony alone.

How well they had taught the lesson—how enduringly they had impressed upon the pliable little mind that she was an intrusion into their lives. How unfortunately typical they are of many parents who unwittingly, unconsciously, merely endure their children.

Contemplate these words from the Gospel of St. Mark: "And they brought young children to him, that he should touch them: and his disciples rebuked those that brought them.

"But when Jesus saw it, he was much displeased, and said unto them, Suffer the little children to come unto me, and forbid them not: for of such is the kingdom of God" (Mark 10:13–14).

A Sacred Influence

While the responsibility to guide little children belongs to both parents, motherhood carries with it a special, sacred influence. The program of The Church of Jesus Christ of Latter-day Saints will not preempt your privileges, Mother. It is structured to strengthen you as a mother. None of it is calculated to diminish your influence in the home. But since there are good mothers—and better mothers—it is patterned to strengthen the very quality of your motherhood. There is a "home partnership" spirit in all that is done. How important it is that every mother teach the principles of life and salvation to her little ones.

It is a common practice for parents to purchase insurance policies and open savings accounts that their children may attend college or fulfill missions. It is generally a good thing to do. But mothers, in all of your looking into the future, you may do well to look to the present. For premiums must be paid on character, too, not just monthly or quarterly or semiannually but moment by moment, day by day, year in, year out. Character must be built little by little "giving line upon line, precept upon precept; here a little, and there a little" (D&C 128:21).

Teaching the Gospel to Children

It is not always a solemn and sobering obligation, this teaching of the gospel to the little children; they have a way of making it pleasant. One mother in South Carolina told me of her youngster who was contesting with a neighbor child over the question, "Which is the only true church?" Her child finally said, "Well, we have a prophet at the head of our Church." The other child conceded finally with the thought, "I guess ours is a non-profit organization."

There is a trend in the world today—and unfortunately in the Church—for women to want to be emancipated. And we wonder at times—emancipated from what? From domesticity? From motherhood? From happiness? And to what are you in slavery? Your children? It is neither necessary nor desirable for the mother of little children to become a drudge or to be relegated to a position of servitude. It is not, however, uncommon to see women—interestingly enough many in the financially well-to-do category—over-surfeiting themselves with activities outside of the home at the expense of their little children.

I have never known a mother to regret in the closing years of her life a sacrifice made for her children or to begrudge the cost of guiding them to fine Christian citizenship.

On the other hand, we find almost universal remorse for neglect of family in the growing years or for overindulging children, which is symptomatic of the most serious type of neglect.

Mothers, do not abandon your responsibilities! Be reverently grateful for your little children.

For Children Impaired

To mothers who have little children who are handicapped, children whose little bodies were born incompletely formed or whose little minds are limited: No one knows the depth of agony that you have suffered. By way of consolation, consider these verses from the Doctrine and Covenants:

"Ye cannot behold with your natural eyes, for the present time, the design of your God concerning those things which shall come hereafter, and the glory which shall follow after much tribulation.

"For after much tribulation come the blessings. Wherefore the day cometh that ye shall be crowned with much glory; the hour is not yet, but is nigh at hand" (D&C 58:3–4).

I suggest that blessings will be extended to mothers such as you who have given tender and affectionate love to handicapped children. Trials such as these bring a reverence for life, a new depth of compassion and motherhood.

For Fostered Children

There are lovely mothers, also, who have fostered children borne by other women. To such the privilege of motherhood is twicefold more precious. And there are many mothers whose love extends beyond their own family. In elementary school I learned a great lesson in this regard. There were in that school several youngsters from a family which was not blessed with an attentive mother at home.

During the school year they were afflicted with impetigo, a common disease of the skin which is now very easily cured. Because they were not bathed and because their clothing was not clean, it quickly spread across their bodies.

The principal of the school asked that my mother, who was the room mother for our class, visit the home in the hope that she could encourage the type of care that these children so badly needed. "The woman's touch," he said, "may be most helpful here."

Although she responded to the request, she failed in her mission, for she found circumstances in that home were pitiable. Well I remember the invitation to bring these little youngsters home from school with us. And I remember that they were bathed; medication was applied to their little bodies; they were dressed in our clothing; and in the early evening sent to their own home, the next day to return for the same treatment. Night after night after night I remember my mother scrubbing endlessly with a bottle of disinfectant and then boiling clothing against the possibility that her own family might become infected. But her mother's heart would not turn them away, for these were little children, and they were suffering.

The demands made upon mothers, the weariness, the worry, the endless vigil—all take their toll. But there comes to you a special beauty transcending even that of the blushing bride. Such beauty is alluded to in these lines by an unknown poet entitled simply "Beauty":

> *Two pines were born on a hillside grove.*
> *One protected, grew straight and tall.*
> *It bore no time or weather marks.*
> *Its figure was slim and virginal.*
> *The second showed clearly that time had passed,*
> *For it stood where the winds stormed by.*
> *Its arms knew the tortuous weight of snow.*
> *Its face knew the sting of the sleet-filled sky.*
> *The first tree, so youthfully beautiful*
> *Was a picture the world could all see.*
> *But the artist who climbed to the hillside grove*
> *Always painted the other tree.*

The Sphere of Mother

Mothers, teach your children in the home the principles of the gospel of Jesus Christ. Sustain your husband as patriarch of the home.

Draw from the priesthood home teaching program, from the Relief Society, and the other auxiliary agencies of the Church the assistance to bless your family.

Teach your daughters the essentials of homemaking. Teach them to be virtuous. Train your sons for service in the mission field. Teach them to be worthy. Teach them to know that the President of the Church is a prophet of God.

It is easy, mothers, for us to love you because, you see, the Lord loves you. Earn, mothers of little children, the witness that Jesus is the Christ, for He lives.

PART FIVE

TEACHERS AND SERVANTS

19

CALLED TO SERVE

> *O suns and skies and clouds of June,*
> *And flowers of June together,*
> *Ye cannot rival for one hour*
> *October's bright blue weather.*
>
> (Helen Hunt Jackson, in *The Best-Loved Poems of the American People* [1936], 566)

Several years ago we were looking for something to inspire a conference of mission presidents. In a very interesting way we found it in a long-unused Primary songbook. The song, entitled "Called to Serve," teaches in a few simple lines the message that I bring to you today.

> *Called to serve Him, heav'nly King of glory,*
> *Chosen e'er to witness for his name,*
> *Far and wide we tell the Father's story,*
> *Far and wide his love proclaim.*

From an address given at general conference, October 4, 1997; see *Ensign*, November 1997, 6–8.

Chorus:
Onward, ever onward, as we glory in his name; . . .
God our strength will be; press forward ever,
Called to serve our King.

Called to know the richness of his blessing—
Sons and daughters, children of a King—
Glad of heart, his holy name confessing,
Praises unto him we bring.

Onward, ever onward, as we glory in his name; . . .
God our strength will be; press forward ever,
Called to serve our King.

(*Hymns,* no. 249)

The willingness of Latter-day Saints to respond to calls to serve is a representation of their desire to do the will of the Lord. That arises from the individual witness that the gospel of Jesus Christ, restored through the Prophet Joseph Smith and contained in the Book of Mormon, is true.

Our baptism is a call to lifelong service to Christ. Like those at the waters of Mormon, we are "baptized in the name of the Lord, as a witness before him that [we] have entered into a covenant with him, that [we] will serve him and keep his commandments, that he may pour out his Spirit more abundantly upon [us]" (Mosiah 18:10).

But the response to calls, to positions, is only a small part of the service given by members of the Church.

I see two kinds of service: one, the service we render when we are called to serve in the Church; the other, the service we willingly give to those around us because we are taught to care.

Over the years I have watched one dear sister give service far beyond any calling to teach or lead in the Church. She sees a need and serves; not "Call me if you need help" but "Here I am; what can I do?" She does so many small things, like holding someone's child in a meeting or taking a child to school who has missed the bus. She always looks for new faces at church and steps forward to make them welcome.

Her husband knows that when they attend a ward social, he can generally count on her saying, "Why don't you go along home. I see they are a little short on help to clear up and do the dishes."

He came home one evening to find her putting the furniture back in place. That morning she had the feeling that she should see how an elderly sister with a heart condition was managing a wedding breakfast for a grandchild who had come from out of state to be married in the temple.

She found the woman sitting alone at the church, in despair, surrounded by the things she had brought in preparation. Somehow there had been a double booking of the hall. In a few hours the guests would arrive. Whatever could she do?

This attentive sister took the older sister home with her and put her down to rest. Then she went to work moving the furniture around. When the guests arrived, a beautiful wedding breakfast was ready to be served.

She learned that spirit of service from her mother. The spirit of service is best taught at home.

We must teach our children by example and tell them that an unselfish spirit is essential to happiness.

"God anointed Jesus of Nazareth with the Holy Ghost and with power," and He "went about doing good" (Acts 10:38). Each one confirmed as a member of the Church has the same gift and the same obligation.

The Lord said, "Behold, it is not meet that I should command in all things; for he that is compelled in all things, the same is a slothful and not a wise servant; wherefore he receiveth no reward" (D&C 58:26).

The Lord said to the Church:

"Verily I say, men should be anxiously engaged in a good cause, and do many things of their own free will, and bring to pass much righteousness;

"For the power is in them, wherein they are agents unto themselves. And inasmuch as men do good they shall in nowise lose their reward.

"But he that doeth not anything until he is commanded, and receiveth a commandment with doubtful heart, and keepeth it with slothfulness, the same is damned" (D&C 58:27–29).

Sometimes because of age or health or the needs of a family, we may not be called to serve. John Milton, the blind poet, wrote, "They also serve who only stand and wait" (John Milton, "On His Blindness," in Charles W. Eliot, ed., *The Harvard Classics* [1937–38], 4:84). To attend, to tithe, and to learn is to serve, and we often speak of serving as a worthy example.

No service in the Church or in the community transcends that given in the home.

The pattern for official callings was established in the early days of the Church. The fifth article of faith teaches "that a man [and for that matter, a woman] must be called of God, by prophecy, and by the laying on of hands by those who are in authority, to preach the Gospel and administer in the ordinances thereof."

It is not in the proper spirit for us to decide where we will serve or where we will not. We serve where we are called. It does not matter what the calling may be.

I was present at a solemn assembly when David O. McKay was sustained as President of the Church. President J. Reuben Clark Jr., who had served as First Counselor to two Presidents, was then sustained as Second Counselor to President McKay. Sensitive to the possibility that some might think that he had been demoted, President Clark said:

"In the service of the Lord, it is not where you serve but how. In The Church of Jesus Christ of Latter-day Saints, one takes the place to which one is duly called, which place one neither seeks nor declines" (Conference Report, April 1951, 154).

When there is a need for someone to serve, the leaders talk about it and pray about it—often more than once. They seek a confirmation from the Spirit, for calls should be made prayerfully and accepted in the same spirit.

There follows an interview to determine worthiness and to explore personal circumstances. No calling is more important nor service more enduring than parenthood. Generally callings in the Church help parents be better parents. Nevertheless, leaders should use both judgment and inspiration to make certain that a call does not make it measurably difficult for parents to serve as parents.

One who has authority to issue a call must rely on inspiration to avoid overburdening those who are always willing.

The person being called should be given time to pray about the call so that, despite any feeling of inadequacy, he or she may have a settled feeling.

There is another part of a call which is required by revelation: "It shall not be given to any one to go forth to preach my gospel, or to build up my church, except he be ordained by some one who has authority, and it is known to the church that he has authority and has been regularly ordained by the heads of the church" (D&C 42:11). So that it will be known to the Church who is called to serve, names are presented in an appropriate meeting for a sustaining vote. That vote is not just to approve; it is a commitment to support.

Following the sustaining, there is an ordination or setting apart. The pattern was set in the early Church when the Lord promised, "I will lay my hand upon you by the hand of my servant." He further promised, "You shall receive my Spirit, the Holy Ghost, even the Comforter, which shall teach you the peaceable things of the kingdom" (D&C 36:2).

When leaders set someone apart, they do more than authorize service. They pronounce a blessing. It is a marvelous thing to receive a blessing from the Lord Jesus Christ through the hands of His servants.

That blessing can cause changes in the life of the one called or in the family.

While we do not ask to be released from a calling, if our circumstances change, it is quite in order for us to counsel with those who have issued the call and then let the decision rest with them. Nor should we feel rejected when we are released by the same authority and with the same inspiration by which we were called.

One of the great influences in my life was to work closely for many years with Belle S. Spafford, general president of the Relief Society, surely one of the greatest women of this dispensation.

One day she told me that as a young woman she explained to her bishop that she was willing to serve but preferred a call to teach. The following week she was called as a counselor to the ward Relief Society president. "I did not relish the call," she said. "The bishop had misunderstood." She told him bluntly Relief Society was for old women. Except for the counsel of her husband, she would have refused the call.

Several times she asked to be released. Each time the bishop said he would pray about it.

One night she was seriously injured in an automobile accident. After some time in the hospital, she was recovering at home. A terrible laceration on her face became infected. The worried doctor told her, "We can't touch this surgically; it's too close to the main nerve in your face."

That Sunday night, as the doctor left the Spafford home, the bishop, returning from a late meeting, saw the lights on and stopped in.

Sister Spafford later told me, "In that pathetic condition I tearfully said, 'Bishop, now will you release me?'"

Again he said, "I will pray about it."

When the answer came, it was, "Sister Spafford, I still can't get the feeling that you should be released from Relief Society."

Belle S. Spafford served for forty-six years in the Relief Society, nearly thirty as general president. She was an influence for good in the Church and was respected by women leaders worldwide.

At a meeting of the World Council of Women in Suriname, citing age and failing health, she submitted a letter of resignation as an officer. She showed me their letter of refusal—they needed her wisdom, her strength of character.

She often spoke of being tested in her calling. Perhaps the greatest test came when, as a young woman, she learned to respect the power and authority inherent in the priesthood and that an ordinary man serving as bishop can receive direction from the Lord in calling members to serve.

The spirit of service does not come by assignment. It is a feeling that accompanies a testimony of the gospel of Jesus Christ.

The Lord said, "If any man serve me, let him follow me; and where I am, there shall also my servant be: if any man serve me, him will my Father honour" (John 12:26).

"For thus saith the Lord—I, the Lord, am merciful and gracious unto those who fear me, and delight to honor those who serve me in righteousness and in truth unto the end.

"Great shall be their reward and eternal shall be their glory" (D&C 76:5–6).

I bear witness that the power and inspiration of calls is present in the Church. I bear witness that the gospel is true and say God bless you who serve, bless you for what you do, and bless you for what you are!

20

THE LIGHT OF CHRIST

Most members of the Church have a basic understanding of the Holy Ghost. Most have experienced its promptings and understand why the Holy Ghost is called the Comforter.

They know "the Holy Ghost . . . is a personage of Spirit" (D&C 130:22) and a member of the Godhead (see Articles of Faith 1:1).

But many do not know that there is another Spirit—"the light of Christ" (D&C 88:7)—another source of inspiration, which each of us possesses in common with all other members of the human family. If we know about the Light of Christ, we will understand that there is something inside all of us, and we can appeal to that in our desire to share truth.

The Holy Ghost and the Light of Christ are different from each other. While they are sometimes described in the scriptures with the same words, they are two different and distinct entities. It is important for you to know about both of them.

From an address given at a mission presidents' seminar, Provo, Utah, June 22, 2004; see *Ensign*, April 2005, 8–14.

The more we know about the Light of Christ, the more we will understand about life and the more we will have a deep love for all mankind. We will be better teachers and missionaries and parents, and better men and women and children. We will have deeper regard for our brothers and sisters in the Church and for those who do not believe and have not yet had conferred upon them the gift of the Holy Ghost.

The Light of Christ is defined in the scriptures as "the Spirit [which] giveth light to *every* man that cometh into the world" (D&C 84:46; italics added); "the light which is in all things, which giveth life to all things, which is the law by which all things are governed" (D&C 88:13; see also John 1:4–9; D&C 84:45–47; 88:6; 93:9).

And the Light of Christ is also described in the scriptures as "the Spirit of Jesus Christ" (D&C 84:45), "the Spirit of the Lord" (2 Corinthians 3:18; see also Mosiah 25:24), "the Spirit of truth" (D&C 93:26), "the light of truth" (D&C 88:6), "the Spirit of God" (D&C 46:17), and "the Holy Spirit" (D&C 45:57). Some of these terms are also used to refer to the Holy Ghost.

The First Presidency has written, "There is a universally diffused essence which is the light and the life of the world, 'which lighteth every man that cometh into the world,' 'which proceedeth forth from the presence of God' throughout the immensity of space, the light and power of which God bestows in different degrees to 'them that ask him,' according to their faith and obedience" (*Improvement Era,* March 1916, 460).

Regardless of whether this inner light, this knowledge of right and wrong, is called the Light of Christ, moral sense, or conscience, it can direct us to moderate our actions—unless, that is, we subdue it or silence it.

Every spirit child of our Heavenly Father enters into mortality to receive a physical body and to be tested.

"The Lord said . . . they are the workmanship of mine own hands, and I gave unto them their knowledge, in the day I created them; and in the Garden of Eden, gave I unto man his agency" (Moses 7:32).

"Wherefore, men are free according to the flesh; and all things are given them which are expedient unto man. And they are free to choose liberty and eternal life, through the great Mediator of all men, or to choose captivity and death, according to the captivity and power of the devil" (2 Nephi 2:27).

Therefore, we know that "every man may act in doctrine and principle pertaining to futurity, according to the *moral agency* [the words *free agency* do not appear in the revelations] which I have given unto him, that every man may be accountable for his own sins in the day of judgment" (D&C 101:78; italics added).

We are admonished to "quench not the Spirit" (1 Thessalonians 5:19). Thus we can see that "[all] are instructed sufficiently that they know good from evil" (2 Nephi 2:5; see also 2 Nephi 2:27). They have their agency, and they are accountable.

This Spirit of Christ fosters everything that is good, every virtue (see Moroni 7:16). It stands in brilliant, indestructible opposition to anything that is coarse or ugly or profane or evil or wicked (see Moroni 7:17).

Conscience affirms the reality of the Spirit of Christ in man. It affirms, as well, the reality of good and evil, of justice, mercy, honor, courage, faith, love, and virtue, as well as the necessary opposites—hatred, greed, brutality, jealousy (see 2 Nephi 2:11, 16). Such values, though physically intangible, respond to laws with cause-and-effect relationships as certain as any resulting from physical laws (see Galatians 6:7–9). Conscience can be likened unto a "guardian angel" for every person (see Joseph Fielding Smith, *Doctrines of Salvation,* comp. Bruce R. McConkie, 3 vols. [1954–56], 1:54).

The Spirit of Christ can enlighten the inventor, the scientist, the painter, the sculptor, the composer, the performer, the architect, the author to produce great, even inspired things for the blessing and good of all mankind.

This Spirit can prompt the farmer in his field and the fisherman on his boat. It can inspire the teacher in the classroom, the missionary in presenting his discussion. It can inspire the student who listens. And of enormous importance, it can inspire husband and wife, and father and mother.

This inner Light can warn and guard and guide. But it can be repulsed by anything that is ugly or unworthy or wicked or immoral or selfish.

The Light of Christ existed in you before you were born (see D&C 93:23, 29–30), and it will be with you every moment that you live and will not perish when the mortal part of you has turned to dust. It is ever there.

Every man, woman, and child of every nation, creed, or color—everyone, no matter where they live or what they believe or what they do—has within them the imperishable Light of Christ. In this respect, all men are created equally. The Light of Christ in everyone is a testimony that God is no respecter of persons (see D&C 1:35). He treats everyone equally in that endowment with the Light of Christ.

It is important for a teacher or a missionary or a parent to know that the Holy Ghost can work through the Light of Christ. A teacher of gospel truths is not planting something foreign or even new into an adult or a child. Rather, the missionary or teacher is making contact with the Spirit of Christ already there. The gospel will have a familiar "ring" to them. Then the teaching will come "to the convincing of [those who will listen] that Jesus is the Christ, the Eternal God, manifesting himself unto all nations" (Book of Mormon, title page).

During His mortal ministry, Jesus taught His gospel and put in place the foundation upon which His Church would be built. The foundation was built of stones of doctrine which can neither be seen with mortal eyes nor felt by touch; they are invisible and intangible.

They will not weather away or crumble. They cannot be broken or dissolved or destroyed. These stones of doctrine are imperishable and indestructible.

These stones of doctrine existed "before the world was" (D&C 124:38), "from before the foundation of the world" (D&C 124:41). Christ built His Church upon them.

Jesus spoke of "the stone which the builders rejected" (Matthew 21:42). Then the shadow of apostasy settled over the earth. The line of priesthood authority was broken. But mankind was not left in total darkness or completely without revelation or inspiration. The idea that with the Crucifixion of Christ the heavens were closed and that they opened in the First Vision is not true. The Light of Christ would be everywhere present to attend the children of God; the Holy Ghost would visit seeking souls. The prayers of the righteous would not go unanswered.

The conferring of the *gift* of the Holy Ghost would await the restoration of the priesthood and the dispensation of the fulness of times when all things would be revealed. Temple work—ordinance work—would then be revealed. Then those who lived during the many generations when essential ordinances were unavailable, when baptism was not available, would be redeemed. God never abandons His children. He never has abandoned this earth.

When the fulness of His gospel was restored, The Church of Jesus Christ of Latter-day Saints was built upon the same foundation stones of doctrine.

Because we learn most everything through physical senses, teaching intangible doctrines which cannot be seen or felt becomes very difficult. Jesus, the Master Teacher, taught these doctrines, and they can be taught in the same way today. It is my purpose to show you how He, the Master Teacher, taught them.

You can come to understand spiritual truths as clearly as if these stones of doctrine were as tangible as granite or flint or marble. Marble will yield to the hands of the sculptor so that others can see what he sees hidden within the shapeless stone. In like manner, you can teach others to see—that is, to understand—these intangible, invisible stones of doctrine.

The way the Savior taught, and the way you can teach, is both simple and very profound. If you choose a tangible object as a symbol for a doctrine, you can teach just as He did. A teacher can associate the doctrine with an object already known, which *can* be seen with physical eyes.

Jesus compared faith to a seed, the tiny mustard seed, which can be seen and touched. He told how if the seed is nurtured, it can grow and flourish and become a tree (see Luke 13:19).

He compared the kingdom of heaven to an everyday object that can be seen. "The kingdom of heaven," He said, "is like unto a net, that was cast into the sea, and gathered of every kind" (Matthew 13:47); and He said, "The kingdom of heaven is like unto treasure hid in a field; the which when a man hath found, he hideth, and for joy thereof goeth and selleth all that he hath, and buyeth that field" (Matthew 13:44).

Christ used as examples, as symbols, such ordinary things as salt (see Matthew 5:13; Mark 9:49–50; Luke 14:34) and candles (see Matthew 5:15; Mark 4:21; Luke 8:16; 11:33–36; Revelation 18:23), as rain (see Matthew 7:25–27) and rainbows (see Revelation 4:3; 10:1). The four Gospels are full of such examples. Likewise the Book of Mormon, the Doctrine and Covenants, and the Pearl of Great Price have dozens of similar references. They are everywhere. That is what a story or a parable is—a true-to-life example used to teach a principle or a doctrine that is invisible or intangible.

One time in Matthew, one time in Luke, four times in the Book of Mormon, and three times in the Doctrine and Covenants, the Savior spoke of a hen with her chicks (see Matthew 23:37; Luke 13:34; 3 Nephi 10:4–6; D&C 10:65; 29:2; 43:24). Everyone knows about hens and chicks, even little children.

Now faith is not really exactly like a seed, nor is the kingdom of heaven exactly like a net or a treasure or leaven (see Luke 13:21) or "a merchant man, seeking goodly pearls" (Matthew 13:45). But with these illustrations, Jesus was able to open the eyes of His disciples—not their natural eyes but the eyes of their understanding (see Matthew 13:15; John 12:40; Acts 28:27; Ephesians 1:18; 2 Nephi 16:10; D&C 76:12, 19; 88:11; 110:1).

With the eyes of our understanding, we see things that are spiritual. With our spirits reaching out, we can touch things that are spiritual and *feel* them. Then we can *see* and we can *feel* things that are invisible to the physical senses. Remember, Nephi told his rebellious brothers, who had rejected a message from an angel, "Ye were past feeling, that ye could not *feel* his words" (1 Nephi 17:45; italics added).

Paul wrote to the Corinthians that "God hath revealed them unto us by his Spirit: for the Spirit searcheth all things, yea, the deep things of God. . . .

"Which things also we speak, not in the words which man's wisdom teacheth, but which the Holy Ghost teacheth; comparing spiritual things with spiritual.

"But the natural man receiveth not the things of the Spirit of God: for they are foolishness unto him: neither can he know them, because they are spiritually discerned" (1 Corinthians 2:10, 13–14).

In modern revelation, Christ spoke of "the light which shineth, which giveth you light [and] enlighteneth your eyes, which is the same light that quickeneth your understandings" (D&C 88:11).

I do not know how to teach about the Spirit of Christ except to follow what the Lord did when He taught invisible, intangible truths to His disciples.

To describe the Light of Christ, I will compare or liken it to the light of the sun. Sunlight is familiar to everyone; it is everywhere present and can be seen and can be felt. Life itself depends upon sunlight.

The Light of Christ *is* like sunlight. It, too, is everywhere present and given to everyone equally.

Just as darkness must vanish when the light of the sun appears, so is evil sent fleeing by the Light of Christ.

There is no darkness in sunlight. Darkness is subject unto it. The sun can be hidden by clouds or by the rotation of the earth, but the clouds will disappear, and the earth will complete its turning.

According to the plan, we are told that "it must needs be, that there is an opposition in all things" (2 Nephi 2:11).

Mormon warned that "the devil . . . persuadeth no man to do good, no, not one; neither do his angels; neither do they who subject themselves unto him.

"[Now] seeing that ye know the light by which ye may judge, which light is the light of Christ, see that ye do not judge wrongfully" (Moroni 7:17–18).

This Light of Christ, which gives life, is within you. The evil one will attempt to obscure it. It can be so clouded with confusion so far as to convince you that it does not even exist.

Just as sunlight is a natural disinfectant, the Spirit of Christ can cleanse the spirit.

Every soul, no matter who or where or when, is a child of God. Our responsibility is to teach that "there is a spirit in man: and the inspiration of the Almighty giveth them understanding" (Job 32:8).

President Joseph Fielding Smith spoke of the teachings of the Holy Ghost and of the Spirit of Christ: "Every man can receive a manifestation of the Holy Ghost, even when he is out of the Church, if he is earnestly seeking for the light and for the truth. The Holy Ghost will come and give the man the testimony he is seeking, and then withdraw; and the man does not have a claim upon another visit or constant visits and manifestations from him. He may have the constant guidance of that other Spirit, the Spirit of Christ" (*Doctrines of Salvation,* 1:42; see also Joseph Smith, *Teachings of the Prophet Joseph Smith,* sel. Joseph Fielding Smith [1976], 149).

The Spirit of Christ is always there. It never leaves. It cannot leave.

Everyone everywhere already has the Spirit of Christ, and while the Spirit of the Holy Ghost can visit anyone, the *gift* of the Holy Ghost is obtained "by obedience to the laws and ordinances of the Gospel" (Articles of Faith 1:3), by submitting to "baptism by immersion for the remission of sins; [and the] laying on of hands for the gift of the Holy Ghost" (Articles of Faith 1:4). It is not automatically present, as the Spirit of Christ is present. This gift must be conferred by one holding authority (see Articles of Faith 1:5).

That is what we are commissioned to do, to foster the Light of Christ, which is within every soul we meet, and bring souls to the point where the Holy Ghost may visit them. And then, in due time, they can receive, through the ordinance, the gift of the Holy Ghost, which is conferred upon every member of the Church.

Once a person has received that gift of the Holy Ghost and can cultivate it together with the Light of Christ, which they already have, then the fulness of the gospel is open to their understanding. The Holy Ghost can even work through the Light of Christ (see Smith, *Doctrines of Salvation,* 1:54).

The Light of Christ is as universal as sunlight itself. Wherever there is human life, there is the Spirit of Christ. Every living soul is possessed of it. It is the sponsor of everything that is good. It is the inspirer of everything that will bless and benefit mankind. It nourishes goodness itself.

Mormon taught, "Search diligently in the light of Christ that ye may know good from evil; and if ye will lay hold upon every good thing, and condemn it not, ye certainly will be a child of Christ" (Moroni 7:19).

Everyone knows about sunlight. When you liken the Spirit of Christ to sunlight, ordinary examples from your own experiences may come to your mind. These examples are almost endless. These examples can be understood by little children or by adults, as the parables of Christ can be understood. It should not be difficult to teach how revelation can come through Light, even though we do not know exactly how inspiration works.

Man himself, with all his limitations, can convey messages through fiber-optic cables. A single tiny fiber of glass, smaller than a human hair, can carry 40,000 messages at the same time. These can then be decoded and turned into sight and sound and color, even motion. Man can do that.

A laser beam, where there is no wire or fiber at all, can carry 100 billion bits of information in a second.

If man can do that, why should we marvel at the promise that the Light of Christ is in all of us and that the Holy Ghost can visit any of us?

It should not be difficult, therefore, to understand how revelation from God to His children on earth can come to all mankind through both the Spirit of Christ and the Holy Ghost.

This Light of Christ is everywhere in the scriptures. The Doctrine and Covenants is a very rich source of teaching on the Light of Christ. For example, it speaks of "the light of truth; which truth shineth. This is the light of Christ. . . . He is in the sun, and the light of the sun, and the power thereof by which it was made" (D&C 88:6–7).

Ordinary teachers responsible to teach the doctrines and to testify of spiritual things have within their own personal experience everyday things which can be likened unto things which are spiritual.

Then the Light of Christ can be ignited by the Spirit of the Holy Ghost, the Comforter. We are told that then "the Comforter, which is the Holy Ghost, whom the Father will send in my name, he shall teach you all things, and bring all things to your remembrance, whatsoever I have said unto you" (John 14:26).

President Harold B. Lee explained: "That light never entirely goes out . . . [speaking of the Light of Christ] unless we commit the unpardonable sin. Its glow may be so dim that we can hardly perceive it, but it is there for us to fan into a flame that shall burn brighter with understanding and with knowledge. Except for that, we wouldn't be able to achieve. Our missionary work would come to naught" (*The Teachings of Harold B. Lee,* ed. Clyde J. Williams [1996], 101).

If we understand the reality of the Light of Christ in everyone we see and in every meeting we attend and within ourselves and understand the great challenge that we have—the surroundings in which we live, the danger which sometimes besets us—we will have courage and inspiration beyond that which we have known heretofore. And it *must* be so! And it *will* be so! All of this is a dimension of gospel truth that too few understand.

May you prayerfully and diligently endeavor to comprehend the meaning of these principles and then begin to apply them. As you do, then follows the testimony that the gospel of Jesus Christ is true, that the restoration of the gospel is a reality, and that The Church of Jesus Christ of Latter-day Saints is "the only true and living church upon the face of the whole earth" (D&C 1:30). Jesus is the Christ, the Son of God, the Only Begotten of the Father. And from Him emanates the Light of Christ to all mankind.

May you who are called as missionaries or teachers and you who are parents "feast upon the words of Christ; for behold, the words of Christ will tell you all things what ye should do" (2 Nephi 32:3).

21

GIFTS OF THE SPIRIT

I wonder if you would fancy that I am a teacher and if we both could fancy that this is a classroom instead of this large auditorium, so that I might give my presentation a little differently than usual. I may shuffle back and forth through some papers, referring to some scriptures, reading some of them in full, and in others just touching a word or two.

I begin with section 46, verse 2, of the Doctrine and Covenants. It will outline what I hope we can comply with this evening in relation to meetings and the Spirit: "But notwithstanding those things which are written, it always has been given to the elders of my church from the beginning, and ever shall be, to conduct all meetings as they are directed and guided by the Holy Spirit."

Section 46 is a special section. The subject of that section is the *gifts of the Spirit,* and that is our subject. The *gifts of the Spirit* are sacred, and I approach the subject with reverence, for we are counseled in the scriptures that we should not speak lightly of sacred things.

From an address given at a sixteen-stake fireside, Brigham Young University, January 4, 1987.

What Are the Gifts of the Spirit?

There are three quite comprehensive listings of these gifts in the scriptures, interestingly enough one each in the Bible, the Book of Mormon, and the Doctrine and Covenants. I'd like to touch on a word or phrase here and there, hoping that you will see the similarities and understand something of the words that are emphasized.

From the Bible:

"Now there are *diversities of gifts,* but the *same Spirit.*

"And there are *differences of administrations,* but the *same Lord.*

"And there are diversities of operations, but it is the same God which worketh all in all.

"But the manifestation of the Spirit is given *to every man to profit withal*" (1 Corinthians 12:4–7; italics added).

Now we know two things: there is a diversity of gifts of the Spirit, and they are given to all men "to profit withal." This list mentions the word of wisdom, the word of knowledge, the gift of faith, the gifts of healing, working of miracles, prophecy, and other gifts:

"For to one is given by the Spirit the *word of wisdom;* to another the *word of knowledge* by the same Spirit;

"To another *faith* by the same Spirit; to another the *gifts of healing* by the same Spirit:

"To another the *working of miracles;* to another *prophecy;* to another *discerning of spirits;* to another *divers kinds of tongues;* to another the *interpretation of tongues:*

"But all these worketh that one and the selfsame Spirit, dividing to every man severally as he will.

"For as the body is one, and hath many members, and all the members of that one body, being many, are one body: so also is Christ" (1 Corinthians 12:8–12; italics added).

From the Book of Mormon:

"And again, I exhort you, my brethren, that ye deny not the gifts of God, for *they are many;* and they come from the *same God.*"

It then mentions that there are different ways that these gifts are administered, but "it is the same God who worketh all in all." Again, it mentions that one may teach the word of wisdom, another the word of knowledge by the same Spirit, and another may have exceedingly great faith. Then it mentions healing, miracles, and prophecy, the beholding of angels and ministering spirits. It mentions tongues and the interpretation of tongues:

"And there are *different ways* that these gifts are administered; but it is the same God who worketh all in all; and they are given by the manifestations of the Spirit of God *unto men,* to profit them.

"For behold, to one is given by the Spirit of God, that he may *teach the word of wisdom;*

"And to another, that he may *teach the word of knowledge* by the same Spirit;

"And to another, *exceedingly great faith;* and to another, the *gifts of healing* by the same Spirit;

"And again, to another, that he may *work mighty miracles;*

"And again, to another, that he may *prophesy* concerning all things;

"And again, to another, the *beholding of angels and ministering spirits;*

"And again, to another, *all kinds of tongues;*

"And again, to another, the *interpretation of languages* and of divers kinds of tongues."

And then we read this very significant verse:

"And all these gifts come by the Spirit of Christ; and they come unto *every man* severally, according as he will." I believe that "he" refers to us, meaning that the gifts will be received as we will.

And then Moroni said, "And I would exhort you, my beloved brethren, that ye remember that every good gift cometh of Christ" (Moroni 10:8–18; italics added).

From section 46 of the Doctrine and Covenants:

"And again, verily I say unto you, I would that ye should always remember, and always retain in your minds what those gifts are, that are given unto the church.

"For all have not every gift given unto them; for there are *many gifts,* and to *every man* is given a gift by the Spirit of God.

"To some is given one, and to some is given another, that all may be profited thereby.

"To some it is given *by the Holy Ghost* to know *that Jesus Christ is the Son of God,* and that he was crucified for the sins of the world.

"To others it is given to *believe on their words,* that they also might have eternal life if they continue faithful.

"And again, to some it is given by the Holy Ghost *to know the differences of administration,* as it will be pleasing unto the same Lord, according as the Lord will, suiting his mercies according to the conditions of the children of men.

"And again, it is given by the Holy Ghost to some to *know the diversities of operations,* whether they be of God, that the manifestations of the Spirit may be given to *every man* to profit withal.

"And again, verily I say unto you, to some is given, by the Spirit of God, the *word of wisdom.*

"To another is given the *word of knowledge,* that all may be taught to be wise and to have knowledge.

"And again, to some it is given *to have faith to be healed;*

"And to others it is given to have *faith to heal.*

"And again, to some is given the *working of miracles;*

"And to others it is given *to prophesy;*

"And to others the *discerning of spirits.*

"And again, it is given to some to *speak with tongues;*

"And to another is given the *interpretation of tongues.*

"And all these gifts come from God, for the benefit of the children of God" (D&C 46:10–26; italics added).

Several verses later, we read:

"He that asketh in the Spirit asketh according to the will of God; wherefore it is done even as he asketh" (D&C 46:30).

Section 46 includes these verses regarding the bishop and elders who are called to preside:

"And unto the bishop of the church, and unto such as God shall appoint and ordain to watch over the church and to be elders unto the church, are to have it given unto them *to discern all those gifts* lest there shall be any among you professing and yet be not of God.

"And it shall come to pass that he that asketh in Spirit shall receive in Spirit;

"That unto some it may be given to have *all those gifts,* that there may be a head [I take that to refer to the prophet, who is the head of the Church], in order that every member may be profited thereby.

"He that asketh in the Spirit asketh according to the will of God; wherefore it is done even as he asketh" (D&C 46:27–30).

The concluding verses of section 46 admonish us to give thanks unto God for the blessings we receive:

"And again, I say unto you, all things must be done in the name of Christ, whatsoever you do in the Spirit;

"And ye must give thanks unto God in the Spirit for whatsoever blessing ye are blessed with.

"And ye must practice virtue and holiness before me continually. Even so. Amen" (D&C 46:27–33; italics added).

The Gifts Are Diverse

Now, you notice that in all three listings there is harmony. They all mention the "diversity of gifts" but the same "Spirit."

I list again the gifts named in those three citations, plus other references in the scriptures (and there are many of them):

- faith
- the gift of prophecy
- the gift of administration

- seeing as seers see
- revelation
- discernment
- visions
- dreams
- visitations
- promptings
- feelings
- sensing whether a decision is right or wrong
- the gift of healing
- warnings
- raising the dead
- the gift of tongues
- the gift of interpretation of tongues
- the gift of translation
- the gift to teach by the Spirit

There is another gift, one that is a little hard to describe, but perhaps we could say that it is the gift to be guided, or the gift of guidance. I think you will know what I mean. When certain events happen—often small events in our lives—that could not possibly be coincidental, we get the impression that there is a power and a source that knew where we would be and what we would be doing. Examples of this gift often happen in family history work, when things just seem to come together. Spiritual gifts also give aid in many other aspects of our lives.

These gifts have always been present in the Church. After listing the gifts that have been manifest, Alma spoke of the responsibility that is ours to give great care to the use of these gifts:

> Having been visited by the Spirit of God;
> having *conversed with angels,* and
> having been *spoken unto by the voice of the Lord;* and
> having the *spirit of prophecy,*

and the *spirit of revelation,*
and also *many gifts,*
the gift of *speaking with tongues,*
and the *gift of preaching,*
and the *gift of the Holy Ghost,*
and the *gift of translation;* . . .

"And now behold I say unto you, that if this people, who have received so many blessings from the hand of the Lord, should transgress contrary to the light and knowledge which they do have, I say unto you that *if this be the case,* that if they should fall into transgression, *it would be far more tolerable for the Lamanites than for them*" (Alma 9:21–23; italics added).

Considering what the Lamanites were like in that day, we know that Alma was issuing a warning.

The *Word* Gift

I must emphasize that the word *gift* is of great significance, for a gift may not be demanded or it ceases to be a gift. It may only be accepted when proffered.

Inasmuch as spiritual gifts truly are gifts, the conditions under which we may receive them are established by Him who offers them to us. Spiritual gifts cannot be forced, for a gift is a gift. They cannot, I repeat, be forced nor bought nor "earned" in the sense that we make some gesture in payment and then expect them to automatically be delivered on our terms.

There are those who seek spiritual gifts with such persistence that instead they move further from them. In their persistence and determination, they place themselves in spiritual danger. Rather, we are to live worthy of the gifts, and they will come according to the will of the Lord.

Brigham Young said something in his day that surely applies to ours:

"There is no doubt, if a person lives according to the revelations given to God's people, he may have the Spirit of the Lord to signify to him his will, to guide and to direct him in the discharge of his duties, in his temporal as well as his spiritual exercises. I am satisfied however, that in this respect, we live far beneath our privileges" (*Discourses of Brigham Young,* sel. John A. Widtsoe [1954], 32).

Spiritual gifts belong to the Church, and their existence is one of the great and abiding testimonies of the truth of the gospel. They really are not optional with the Church. Mormon taught that if they were absent, then "awful is the state of man" (Moroni 7:38).

We are to seek to be worthy to receive these gifts according to the way that the Lord has directed. Now, I say that again—we are to seek for spiritual gifts in the Lord's way.

We Are to Seek for Spiritual Gifts

Paul wrote to the Corinthians, "Now concerning spiritual gifts, brethren, I would not have you ignorant" (1 Corinthians 12:1).

There are many, many other references, and I will read just a few:

"And again I would exhort you that ye would come unto Christ, and *lay hold upon every good gift,* and touch not the evil gift, nor the unclean thing" (Moroni 10:30; italics added).

Another: "But covet earnestly the best gifts" (1 Corinthians 12:31).

I define *covet* in that frame of reference as to "ardently desire" them in a righteous way.

Then: "Follow after charity, and *desire spiritual gifts*" (1 Corinthians 14:1; italics added).

"Charity," Mormon defined, "is the pure love of Christ" (Moroni 7:47). Often we look at that from the wrong direction. We think the pure love of Christ would be a marvelous thing for us to receive, and we hardly ever think that it is an obligation that we are to give. But read that properly: "Follow after charity, and desire spiritual gifts."

Another reference: "Even so ye, forasmuch as ye are *zealous of spiritual gifts, seek that ye may excel to the edifying of the church*" (1 Corinthians 14:12; italics added).

The second verse of the 46th section of the Doctrine and Covenants gives the instruction to conduct all meetings as we are directed by the Spirit: "But notwithstanding those things which are written, it *always* has been given to the elders of my church *from the beginning,* and *ever shall be,* to conduct *all meetings* as they are *directed* and *guided* by *the Holy Spirit*" (italics added).

A verse in Moroni in the Book of Mormon says the same thing: "And their meetings were conducted by the church after the manner of the workings of the Spirit, and by the power of the Holy Ghost; for as the power of the Holy Ghost led them whether to *preach,* or to *exhort,* or to *pray,* or to *supplicate,* or to *sing,* even so it was done" (Moroni 6:9; italics added).

Notice the words "to sing." There is much to be said about the gifts of the Spirit and music.

Signs to Follow the Believers

The signs will follow those that believe. That is another frequent theme in scripture:

"And he said unto them, Go ye into all the world, and preach the gospel to every creature.

"He that believeth and is baptized shall be saved; but he that believeth not shall be damned.

"And *these signs shall follow them that believe;* In my name shall they *cast out devils;* they shall *speak with new tongues;*

"They shall *take up serpents;* and if they *drink any deadly thing, it shall not hurt them:* they shall lay hands on the *sick,* and they *shall recover*" (Mark 16:15–18; italics added).

And listen very carefully to this verse: "Verily, verily, I say unto you, He that believeth on me, the works that I do shall he do also; and greater works than these shall he do; because I go unto my Father" (John 14:12).

Do Not Seek After Signs—a Definition of Terms

We have the assignment to seek after spiritual gifts, with the very clear notice that signs will follow those that believe. The scriptural direction that we should seek after spiritual gifts and that these signs would follow those that believe has a very important counterbalance, for, by warnings that are unmistakable, we are told not to seek after the signs.

I would like to give something of a definition of my own to the two terms *spiritual gifts* and *signs.*

A spiritual gift is an endowment of spiritual power. For example, the gift of faith or gift of discernment, neither of which may be visible, are spiritual gifts.

Signs, on the other hand, *are evidences, or visible manifestations, that a spiritual power is present.* Signs would include visible miracles, such as healing or raising one from the dead.

The scriptures make it clear that we are *not* to seek after signs, and many references explain that spiritual gifts and the signs which follow them are a product of *faith* and that faith is *not* an outgrowth of the signs. Let me repeat that: Spiritual gifts and the signs that follow them are the product of faith, not the reverse—faith is not an outgrowth of the signs. If we misunderstand this, surely we place ourselves in spiritual jeopardy.

In four places in the Bible, and in several other places, is this very clear statement:

"An evil and adulterous generation seeketh after a sign; and there shall no sign be given to it, but the sign of the prophet Jonas" (Matthew 12:39; 16:4; Mark 8:12; Luke 11:29).

And in the Doctrine and Covenants:

"And he that seeketh signs shall see signs, but not unto salvation.

172

"Verily, I say unto you, there are those among you who seek signs, and there have been such even from the beginning;

"But, behold, *faith cometh not by signs,* but *signs follow those that believe.*

"Yea, signs come by faith, not by the will of men, nor as they please, but by the will of God" (D&C 63:7–10; italics added).

The Lord said, "Wherefore, I, the Lord, am *not pleased* with those among you who have sought after signs and wonders for faith, and not for the good of men unto my glory" (D&C 63:12; italics added).

Be Not Deceived

We speak often of angels and visitations, and we should keep in mind that Moroni taught that there are angels of the adversary. There are forty-six references in the scriptures to evil or unclean spirits. We must stay spiritually attuned, as attested by Moroni (see Ether 8:24–26; Moroni 10:7–8).

"Wherefore, beware lest ye are deceived: and that *ye may not be deceived; seek ye earnestly the best gifts,* always remembering for what they are given" (D&C 46:8; italics added).

"But ye are commanded in all things to ask of God, who giveth liberally; and that which the Spirit testifies unto you even so I would that ye should do in all holiness of heart, walking uprightly before me, considering the end of your salvation, doing all things with prayer and thanksgiving, that ye may not be *seduced by evil spirits, or doctrines of devils, or the commandments of men;* for some are of men, and others of devils" (D&C 46:7; italics added).

Occasionally, we find someone who claims to receive spiritual revelations. One of the evidences of false revelation we had better be careful of is that these persons begin to act as though they are receiving spiritual instruction for others. They seem to think somehow that the inspiration they receive supersedes that which the bishops or stake presidents might receive and comes from some higher source than these brethren are privileged to have.

Some are deceived, and endless mischief and sorrow occur. The destructive result of being misled is twofold. Those who have been misled may become afraid, thinking that they themselves might misunderstand spiritual promptings or go "too far." As a result, they hold back and submerge the spiritual part of their lives. Then, for fear of going too far, they avoid the very spiritual feelings that can correctly lead them and make them worthy to receive true spiritual gifts.

If we are not well-grounded in spiritual matters, we tend to draw back and lose *trust* and *faith*. Remember, faith is the one essential prerequisite to receiving spiritual gifts. When we lose faith or are hesitant to exercise faith, the Church is weakened and the progress of the work is affected.

Now there is one way to protect ourselves from this. The key is given to us in section 46. It is a verse of vital importance, and I will read it twice.

"And unto the bishop of the church, and unto such as God shall appoint and ordain to watch over the church and to be elders unto the church, are to have it given unto them to discern all those gifts lest there shall be any among you professing and yet be not of God" (D&C 46:27).

Let me read that again. You bishops and you elders, including stake presidents, pay particular attention because this is part of your assignment: "And unto the bishop of the church, and unto such as God shall appoint and ordain to watch over the church and to be elders unto the church, are to have it given unto them to discern all those gifts lest there shall be any among you professing and yet be not of God" (D&C 46:27).

And verse 29 reads: "That unto some it may be given to have all those gifts, that there may be a head, in order that every member may be profited thereby" (D&C 46:29).

The "head," of course, refers to the prophet and president of the

Church. He has the right and authority to exercise all of the keys and is able to receive all of the gifts that there might "be a head, in order that every member may be profited thereby."

The key is to follow the counsel of your bishop and those elders who are ordained to watch over the Church. Then you will be safe. If someone pretends to be receiving revelations that include you, that "spiritual gift" does not come from the right source. Flee from it with all speed.

There is *great* purpose in teaching the lines of authority and the patterns of protocol in priesthood government. Sometimes members get a little weary of that, but there is a great and powerful protection in it.

Protection is embodied in a word that is very unpopular, particularly when we are young: obedience! We need to understand the order of the priesthood and the *safety in following the counsel of priesthood leaders.* Then, if someone should try to mislead us, our bishop or stake president can counsel us, and if we have the right spirit, we will obediently follow, and all will be well with us.

I do not know of any case where a member who has been misled would not have been protected had they followed the counsel of their bishop. Invariably, they received counsel but turned aside from it, thinking that their inspiration took precedence. I repeat, there is great protection in following the counsel of our local leaders if we desire to qualify for spiritual gifts.

Spiritual Gifts Are a Product of Faith

Spiritual gifts, I repeat, are a product of our faith, and if we don't have them, something is less than it should be. Listen to this prophecy of Mormon:

"And now, my beloved brethren, if this be the case that these things [miracles and faith] are true which I have spoken unto you, and God will show unto you, *with power and great glory at the last day* that they are true, and if they are true has the day of miracles ceased?" Did you notice that he said "the last day"?

175

"Or have angels ceased to appear unto the children of men? Or has he withheld the power of the Holy Ghost from them? Or will he, so long as *time shall last,* or the earth shall stand, or there shall be *one man* upon the face thereof to be saved?

"Behold I say unto you, Nay; for it is by *faith* that miracles are wrought; and it is by *faith* that angels appear and minister unto men; [and then he gives this warning:] wherefore, *if these things have ceased wo be unto the children of men,* for it is because of *unbelief,* and all is vain.

"For no man can be saved, according to the words of Christ, save they shall have *faith in his name;* wherefore, if these things have ceased, *then has faith ceased also;* and *awful* is the state of man, for *they are as though there had been no redemption made*" (Moroni 7:35–38; italics added).

It is well to remember the adage that he who *will* not read has no advantage over him who *cannot* read.

If faith has ceased also, "awful is the state of man, for they are as though there had been no redemption made" (Moroni 7:38).

But Mormon was an optimist, because he concluded with this: "But behold, my beloved brethren, I judge better things of you, for I judge that ye have faith in Christ because of your meekness; for if ye have not faith in him then *ye are not fit to be numbered among the people of his church*" (Moroni 7:39; italics added).

Thankfully, those things—spiritual gifts—are with us. We do not talk about them lightly and we do not talk about them often, but they are present with the Saints.

Mormon goes on to explain the special responsibility of those who are called to positions of leadership in the Church, the *chosen vessels* of the Lord. He said: "Have miracles ceased? Behold I say unto you, Nay; neither have angels ceased to minister unto the children of men.

"For behold, they [the angels] are subject unto him, to minister according to the word of his command, showing themselves unto them of strong faith and a firm mind in every form of godliness" (Moroni 7:29–30).

Then he tells us what the office of an angel is: "And the *office of their ministry* is to call men unto repentance, and to fulfill and to do the work of the covenants of the Father, which he hath made unto the children of men, to prepare the way among the children of men" (Moroni 7:31; italics added).

Then he tells how the angels are to perform "the office of their ministry," "to call men unto repentance, and to fulfil and to do the work of the covenants of the Father, which he hath made unto the children of men": "By declaring the word of Christ *unto the chosen vessels* of the Lord, that they may bear testimony of him" (Moroni 7:31; italics added).

You would do well to learn in your youth to heed the counsel and the testimonies of the chosen vessels of the Lord. "And by so doing," Mormon continues, "the Lord God prepareth the way that the residue of men may have faith in Christ, that the Holy Ghost may have place in their hearts, according to the power thereof; and after this manner bringeth to pass the Father, the covenants which he hath made unto the children of men" (Moroni 7:32).

Receiving Spiritual Gifts Requires Effort and Worthiness

Spiritual gifts do not come lightly or easily. I reverently mention another gift that is referred to in very simple terms: "Blessed are the pure in heart, for they shall see God" (Matthew 5:8).

Doctrine and Covenants 93:1 gives us the requirements for receiving that gift: "Verily, thus saith the Lord: It shall come to pass that every soul who forsaketh his sins and cometh unto me, and calleth on my name, and obeyeth my voice and keepeth my commandments *shall see my face and know that I am*" (italics added).

Doctrine and Covenants 88:68 reveals more: "Therefore, sanctify yourselves that your minds become single to God, and the days will come *that you will see him;* for he will *unveil his face* unto you, and it shall be in *his* own time and in *his* own way and according to *his* own will" (italics added).

The scriptures teach us about those things that are deterrents to the reception of spiritual gifts. Of course, transgression and wickedness are obvious obstacles. They short-circuit the possibility of receiving spiritual gifts. Apathy and indifference or being caught up too much in the things of the world are also deterrents.

Relying on Intellect

There is another matter that you ought to have somewhere in your consciousness, one that particularly applies to a university setting. It is that we can rely too much on our intellect, on our minds. Now, our "thinkers" are necessary and we need to use them. But we also need to learn to *feel* a few things.

Do you remember the lesson the Lord taught Oliver Cowdery when he was trying to translate? He thought the answers would just be given to him. The Lord said, in effect, "You needed to use your mind first; you needed to use your intellect first. You were to study it out, and then the spiritual element would have been there."

We must keep those sensitive feelings as a vital part of our lives.

You remember the incident in 1 Nephi where Laman and Lemuel were abusing Nephi unmercifully. He said to them, in effect, "I can't understand you":

"Ye are swift to do iniquity but slow to remember the Lord your God. Ye have seen an angel, and he spake unto you; yea, ye have heard his voice from time to time; and he hath spoken unto you in a still small voice, but ye were past *feeling,* that ye could not *feel* his words" (1 Nephi 17:45; italics added).

How Do We Prepare to Receive the Gifts of the Spirit?

As we prepare to receive spiritual gifts, we must remember that they cannot be forced. Music, for example, is a powerful tool in setting the stage for the reception of spiritual things. Of course, it must be the right kind with the right spirit. There is much more that could be said regarding music and the Spirit.

Spiritual Gifts Carry Great Responsibility

Spiritual gifts carry great responsibility, and we are not to talk about them lightly. I see no purpose, for instance, of chattering endlessly about evil spirits. Missionaries and even returned missionaries are somehow wont to do that. There is no purpose in that. I would not do it. And I wouldn't stay in a place where it is happening. Do not sit around and talk about the so-called experiences of those who have confronted evil spirits.

I have always felt that deep spiritual experiences are very personal and very private. Sometimes people wonder why the Brethren do not talk more about their spiritual experiences and have therefore assumed that we do not have them. That is a very erroneous assumption. We have simply read what Alma said:

"It is given unto many to know the mysteries of God; nevertheless they are laid under a strict command that they shall not impart only according to the portion of his word which he doth grant unto the children of men, according to the heed and diligence which they give unto him" (Alma 12:9).

The Consummate, Supernal Spiritual Gift

Now I would speak of the supernal, consummate, spiritual gift! It is so simple and so often present that we often ignore it. It is almost overwhelming when you come to understand that the Holy Ghost, when it is conferred, is a *gift!* Now, those outside of the Church may be influenced by the Holy Ghost, may be inspired by it. That must be true, or else how could they receive the inspiration to be converted? But at baptism we have conferred upon us the gift of the Holy Ghost as a presence.

I quote from Moses: "And he also said unto him: If thou wilt turn unto me, and *hearken* unto my voice, and *believe,* and *repent* of all thy transgressions, and *be baptized,* even in water, in the name of mine Only Begotten Son, who is full of grace and truth, which is Jesus Christ, the only name which shall be given under heaven, whereby salvation shall come unto the children of men, ye shall receive the *gift of the Holy Ghost,* asking all things in his name, and whatsoever ye shall ask, it shall be given you" (Moses 6:52; italics added).

And in the Doctrine and Covenants: "Yea, behold, I will tell you *in your mind* and *in your heart,* by the Holy Ghost, which shall come upon you and which shall dwell in your heart" (D&C 8:2; italics added).

This is the supernal gift, the one that each one of us has access to if we will.

Angels speak by the power of the Holy Ghost. Nephi, after talking along these same lines, chided some of his listeners:

"Wherefore, now after I have spoken these words, *if ye cannot understand them it will be because ye ask not, neither do ye knock; wherefore, ye are not brought into the light, but must perish in the dark.*

"For behold, again I say unto you that if ye will enter in by the way, and receive the *Holy Ghost,* it will show unto you all things what ye should do" (2 Nephi 32:4–5; italics added).

Testimony

Here we are as Latter-day Saints, members of The Church of Jesus Christ of Latter-day Saints. We have the gospel. We are pressed going to and fro with the necessities of life, of living in mortality, and that part of our existence is quite in order. In the presence of His Apostles, the Lord prayed for them unto the Father not that they should be taken out of the world but that they should be kept from sin (see John 17:15).

We are not to be of the world; we are to be in the world but not of the world. And in the world we have the right, if we would live for it, to be possessed of that quiet spiritual guidance—if we will not seek for the manifestations of it, if we will not seek after signs. If we will live to be worthy, there will attend us a guiding spirit that, if we are obedient, will preclude our doing anything in mortality that would interfere with our ultimate exaltation and our right to return to the presence of Him who is our Father.

Now, in your mature youth—for you are young adults—do not despise the things of the Spirit; do not set them second after things that are intellectual. Intellectually, we want the evidence, we want the proof, *we seek after the signs!* But it is that spiritual part of our nature, which we must accept on pure faith, that prepares us to receive these supernal gifts.

And I affirm to you, as one who has the right to that witness, that Jesus is the Christ, the Son of God, the Only Begotten of the Father; that these gifts are present with the Church; that angels have not ceased to appear and administer to men, nor will they so long as time shall last or earth shall stand or there shall be one man upon the face thereof to be saved (see Moroni 7:29, 36).

These things have not ceased, for in the Church there is that great power of faith—and it dwells in each one of you. As you say your humble prayers, humbly appeal to the Lord that the gift of faith might be yours for His purposes and that these gifts, if He will, might come to you, that you might serve others.

22

THE PLAY AND
THE PLAN

I speak from the Seattle Institute of Religion rather than from one of our Church schools to demonstrate our equal concern for all the youth of the Church. It is not possible for us to provide schools for all who are worthy and qualified to attend. You are all very precious to the Lord. He will bless you wherever you are as you seek to live the gospel.

In my mind's eye, I can see you—well more than forty thousand of you gathered in many locations. Many of you attend Church schools. Many more of you are enrolled in institutes of religion. You who are not students are equally important, and you are invited to enroll in classes at the institutes of religion.

You are young and I am not. We regard you as Paul did Timothy when he wrote, "Let no man despise thy youth" (1 Timothy 4:12).

David was young when he met Goliath, who, supposing that David was afraid, taunted him, saying, "Come to me."

From an address given at a Church Educational System fireside for college-age young adults, Kirkland, Washington, May 7, 1995.

David answered, in effect, "Wait till I get a little boulder—a smooth one."

Goliath, the scriptures say, "disdained him: for he was but a youth." When David swung his sling, the first solid idea that Goliath ever had soon entered his head.

King Saul had armed David with his helmet of brass and his coat of mail. But "David said unto Saul, I cannot go with these; for I have not proved them. And David put them off him."

A short while later, David said to the Philistine, "Thou comest to me with a sword, and with a spear, and with a shield: but I come to thee in the name of the Lord of hosts" (see 1 Samuel 17:38–49).

Immunization

You young adults have invisible Goliaths—both physical and spiritual—to conquer. You will need to be trained how to protect yourself against them.

When you were children you went through a program of immunization. Antibodies were injected into your system to protect you should you be exposed to contagions—enemies so small as to be invisible.

Until recent years one was required to carry an international certificate of vaccination when traveling abroad. That certificate recorded one's immunization against certain diseases, and one was required to present it with a passport at airline ticket counters. Without it one was not allowed to board a plane destined for some countries.

On one occasion, about midnight, I handed my passport and certificate of vaccination to an agent in Los Angeles. I was told that one immunization had expired, and I would not be allowed to board the flight.

What to do? Upon learning that there was an all-night clinic near the airport, I rushed there by cab, received the injection, had my record stamped, and raced back to catch the plane.

Thereafter I was more careful to check my records. Even though the regulations have loosened up, we still pay sensible attention to protecting ourselves when traveling abroad. I do not know how many times I have been exposed to, yet spared from, serious illness by having submitted to the momentary discomfort of an inoculation.

Immunizing the Spirit

While we can protect our bodies from contagious diseases with the proper serum, we cannot immunize our minds and spirits that way. We immunize our minds and our spirits with *ideas,* with *truth.*

It is my purpose to do just that—to inoculate you with an idea, a truth that, if admitted into your thinking and into the cradle of your feelings, may protect you against wicked spiritual diseases to which you are exposed every day of your lives.

The Great Plan of Happiness

The course of our mortal life, from birth to death, conforms to eternal law and follows a plan described in the revelations as "the great plan of happiness" (Alma 42:8). The one idea, the one truth I would inject into your minds is this: *There are three parts to the plan. You are in the second or the middle part, the one in which you will be tested by temptation, by trials, and perhaps by tragedy.* Understand that, and you will be better able to make sense of life and to resist the disease of doubt and despair and depression.

The Play

The plan of redemption, with its three divisions, might be likened to a grand three-act play. Act I is titled "Premortal Life." The scriptures describe it as our first estate (Jude 1:6; Abraham 3:26, 28). Act II, from birth to resurrection, is titled the "Second Estate." And Act III is titled "Life After Death" or "Eternal Life."

In mortality we are like one who enters a theater just as the curtain goes up on the second act. We have missed Act I. The production has many plots and subplots that interweave, making it difficult to figure out who relates to whom and what relates to what, who are the heroes and who are the villains. It is further complicated because we are not just spectators; we are also members of the cast, on stage, in the middle of it all!

Memory Veiled

Because we are part of the eternal plan, the memory of our premortal life, Act I, is covered with a veil. Since we enter mortality at the beginning of Act II with no recollection of Act I, it is little wonder that it is difficult to understand what is going on.

That loss of memory gives us a clean start. It is ideal for the test; it secures our individual agency and leaves us free to make choices. Many of them must be made on faith alone. Even so, we carry with us some whispered knowledge of our premortal life and our status as offspring of immortal parents.

We were born in innocence, for "every spirit of man was innocent in the beginning" (D&C 93:38). And we have an inborn sense of right and wrong, for the Book of Mormon tells us we "are instructed sufficiently that [we] know good from evil" (2 Nephi 2:5).

We progress or are held back in life within the limits imposed by the spiritual and natural law that governs the entire universe. We sometimes wonder, *if* the plan really *is* the great plan of happiness, then why must we struggle to find the fulness of it in mortal life?

If you expect to find only ease and peace and bliss during Act II, you surely will be frustrated. You will understand little of what is going on and why things are permitted to be as they are.

Remember this: the line *"And they all lived happily ever after"* is *never written into the second act!* That line belongs in the *third* act, when the mysteries are solved and everything is put right. The Apostle Paul was right when he said, "If in this life only we have hope in Christ, we are of all men most miserable" (1 Corinthians 15:19).

Until you have a broad perspective of the eternal nature of this great drama, you won't make much sense out of the inequities in life. Some are born with so much and others with so little—some in poverty and some with handicaps, with pain, with suffering. Even innocent children die prematurely. There are the brutal, unforgiving forces of nature and the brutality of man to man. We've seen a lot of that recently.

Do not suppose that God willfully causes that, which for His own purposes He *permits.* When you know the *plan* and *purpose* of it all, even these things will manifest a loving Father in Heaven.

The Script

There exists something of a script for this great play, the drama of the ages. It outlines, in brief form at least, what happened in Act I, "Premortal Life." While there is not much detail, the script makes clear the purpose of it all. And it reveals enough of the plot to help you figure out what life is all about.

That script, as you should already know, is the *script*-tures, the revelations. Read them, study them. They tell you "what is man," why God is "mindful of him," and why we are made "a little lower than the angels," or as Joseph Smith translated the phrase, a little *less* than the *Gods* (see *Teachings of the Prophet Joseph Smith,* sel. Joseph Fielding Smith [1976], 312), yet "crowned . . . with glory and honour" (Psalm 8:4–5).

The scriptures speak the truth. From them you can learn enough about all three acts to get your bearings and direction in life. They reveal that "ye were also in the beginning with the Father; that which is Spirit, even the Spirit of truth," and that "truth is knowledge of things as they are, and as they were, and as they are to come" (D&C 93:23–24).

You can learn of things as they were, as they actually are (not just as they appear to be), and as they are to come. What happens to us after the curtain comes down on this second act of mortal life we take on faith. Each of us writes our own ending to Act II.

The Plan

I have studied this script, the scriptures, and even memorized parts of it. I'm sure you have also. Let me tell you in brief headlines what the scriptures say about this drama of the ages, *The Great Plan of Happiness.*

The spirits of men and women are eternal (*Teachings,* 157–58, 208; D&C 93:29–31). All are sons and daughters of God and lived in a premortal life as His spirit children (Hebrews 12:9; Numbers 16:22; D&C 76:24). The spirit of each individual is in the likeness of the person in mortality (D&C 77:2), male and female (Abraham 4:27; Moses 6:9, 10; D&C 132:63). All are in the image of heavenly parents.

In the council of the Gods (*Teachings,* 348–49), the plan of "the Eternal God" (Alma 34:9) was sustained. It provided for the creation of an earth (Abraham 3:24) whereupon His children would receive physical bodies (Abraham 4:26–27; Moses 6:3–10, 22, 59) and be tested according to His commandments (Abraham 3:25). Each spirit in premortal life was provided opportunities for learning and obedience. Each was given agency (Alma 13:3–5).

A Grand Council in Heaven was convened (*Teachings,* 357). The divine plan required one to be sent as a Savior and Redeemer to fulfill the plan of the Father. The firstborn of the Eternal Father, Jehovah, willingly volunteered and was chosen (Abraham 3:19, 22–27; Moses 4:1–2).

Most spirits sustained this choice. Others rebelled, and there was a "war in heaven." Satan and those who followed him in rebellion against the Father's plan were cast out and denied mortality (Revelation 12:7–13; Moses 4:3; D&C 29:36; 76:28).

Those who kept the first estate (you are among them) were to be added upon with a physical body and were permitted to live upon the earth in this planned second estate (Abraham 3:26). Each was appointed the "times and the bounds of their habitation" (Acts 17:26; Deuteronomy 32:8). Some were foreordained to be prophets (Abraham 3:23; Alma 13:7–9; *Teachings,* 365).

An earth was then organized (Abraham 5:4). Adam and Eve, in a paradisiacal state, were the first man and first woman (Moses 1:34; 3:7; 4:26; 6:3–10, 22, 59). They were married eternally (Moses 3:23–24) and were given commandments. They were in a state of innocence and knew no sin (2 Nephi 2:23).

Eve, beguiled by Satan (Moses 4:6, 19), transgressed and was to be cast out of the garden. Adam chose to obey the first commandment to multiply and replenish the earth. He, with Eve, was subject to the Fall, which introduced mortality to the earth (Moses 2:28; 3:17; 4:13; Alma 12:22). Adam and Eve became the first parents of the family of all the earth (2 Nephi 21:20).

Angels were sent to reveal to Adam the eternal plan of redemption (Moses 5:4–9; 6:48–62), and an Atonement was wrought by Jesus Christ. Through the Atonement, the effects of the Fall—mortal death and spiritual death—could both be overcome (Alma 42:7–9; Helaman 14:16–18). Christ unconditionally provided a resurrection for all mankind whereby we overcome *physical* death (Helaman 14:15).

But overcoming *spiritual* death, which is separation from God, requires that we obey the laws and ordinances of the gospel of Jesus Christ (Articles of Faith 1:3; *Teachings,* 48).

These principles and ordinances were instituted before the foundation of the world. They are not to be altered or changed. All must be saved by the same requirements (*Teachings,* 58–60, 308, 367). The priesthood administers the ordinances of salvation (*Teachings,* 158). The keys of the priesthood control the use of the priesthood (D&C 27:12–13; 110; *Teachings,* 157).

When you die, you are introduced to the spirit world (*Teachings,* 309–10). It is happiness, a paradise, for the righteous. It is misery for the wicked (Alma 40:7–14; 2 Nephi 9:10–16). In either, we continue to learn and are accountable for our actions (D&C 138:10–22).

After all have been dealt with equally (*Teachings,* 219), a judgment will be rendered (Mosiah 3:18). Each will be resurrected in his or her own order (1 Corinthians 15:21–22). The glory one receives, however, will depend on obedience to the laws and ordinances of our Father's plan (1 Corinthians 15:40–42).

Those who have become pure, through repentance, will obtain eternal life and return to the presence of God. They will be exalted as heirs of God and joint heirs with Christ (D&C 76:94–95; 84:35; 132:19–20; Romans 8:17; *Teachings*, 374).

Provision is made in the plan for those who live in mortality without knowing of the plan. "Where there is no law given there is no punishment; and where there is no punishment there is no condemnation . . . because of the atonement; for they are delivered" (2 Nephi 9:25).

Without the sacred work of the redemption of the dead, the plan would be incomplete and would really be unfair.

The ordinances of the temple, the endowments, the sealing in eternal marriage are worth all the preparation required. Do not do anything that may make you unworthy to receive them, or Act III of this eternal drama will be less than you are now free to make it.

That is a brief overview of this eternal drama as recorded in the scriptures. When you understand it, it will give you purpose and direction in life.

Then you will have your *feet on straight* and your *head on the ground.* (I put that in to see if you are paying attention and also to illustrate that there is humor and enjoyment in life—they are a part of the plan!)

There is, of course, a villain in all this—the adversary, the schemer, the destroyer. He got off track in Act I. He has sworn to spoil the plan for everyone. And he has legions of angels, dark angels, to help him do it. He too has a plan called "that cunning plan" (2 Nephi 9:28), "a very subtle plan" (Alma 12:4), a "secret plan" (Helaman 2:8), "the great plan of destruction" (3 Nephi 1:16).

"He persuadeth no man to do good, no, not one; neither do his angels; neither do they who subject themselves unto him" (Moroni 7:17).

Now, here you are on stage in Act II of this eternal drama, your own second estate. You live in the last days, a dispensation of intense testing and unequaled opportunity. Paul the Apostle wrote a remarkable prophecy to young Timothy. He said, "In the last days perilous times shall come" (2 Timothy 3:1). He described our day in accurate detail.

He wrote of men becoming "lovers of their own selves" (2 Timothy

3:2). He spoke of disobedience to parents, of "despisers of those that are good" (2 Timothy 3:3). He even saw those who, "without natural affection" (2 Timothy 3:3), could abuse little children, and those who now rally in protest for the abandonment of those standards without which civilization will not endure.

Now, when enough people protest limits on conduct, the limits are moved farther out and behavior that was once prohibited is reclassified as moral, legal, and socially acceptable, and people rally and protest to make it so. The bonds of marriage and kinship are seen as bondage rather than as sacred ties. The home and the family, absolutely critical to the plan, are now besieged. And you are on stage in the center of it all.

Just as the air you breathe may expose you to a deadly virus, the thoughts you think may introduce spiritual diseases that, if untreated, may prove spiritually fatal.

But Paul's prophecy of the perilous last days included an antidote—the immunization that can protect, even cure, you. After describing those who are "ever learning, and never able to come to the knowledge of the truth" (2 Timothy 3:7), he counseled:

"But continue thou in the things which thou hast learned and hast been assured of, knowing of whom thou hast learned them." Know who is teaching you.

"And that from a child *thou hast known the holy scriptures,* which are able to make thee wise unto salvation through faith which is in Christ Jesus.

"All scripture is given by inspiration of God, and is profitable for doctrine, for reproof, for correction, for instruction in righteousness" (2 Timothy 3:14–16; italics added).

For example, 1 Nephi, chapter 8, in the Book of Mormon, describes the great and spacious building. Put those verses together with 2 Timothy, chapter 3, from the New Testament, and you will see the world in which you live. Read those scriptures thoughtfully.

You will learn that the plan is fair; however it appears, it is fair. Alma told his son that the commandments were not given until *after* the plan was revealed, saying, "God gave unto them commandments, *after* having made known unto them the plan of redemption" (Alma 12:32; italics added).

The Prophet Joseph Smith taught that "all beings who have bodies have power over those who have not. The devil has no power over us only as we permit him" (*Teachings,* 181).

Lest unwittingly you give him such permission, let me alert you to ideas floating around that are spiritually dangerous. For an example, take the word *freedom.*

Freedom—Agency

A little twisting of the word *freedom* can lead to the loss of it. Individual freedom without responsibility can destroy freedom. For example, there are many who indulge freely in that which the Lord has forbidden, and now, as a result, following—compelled by, I suppose—physical impulses, they are prisoners to an incurable disease, and they expose the innocent as well.

It is in the name of freedom that terrorists now seek to destroy the institutions of society that were established to guarantee freedom. Read the first few verses of Helaman, chapter 12, and you will learn why terror will yet be visited upon mankind. It's interesting to find the word *terror* in the Book of Mormon.

We speak often of *agency* as a divine right. The only agency spoken of in the revelations is *moral* agency! This, the Lord said, is given "that every man may act in doctrine and principle pertaining to futurity, according to the moral agency which I have given unto him, that every man may be accountable for his own sins in the day of judgment" (D&C 101:78). If you do not temper freedom with responsibility and agency with accountability, they both will self-destruct.

Diversity

Here's another example: diversity is a very popular word that self-destructs if handled carelessly. Properly respected, diversity is friend to the word *choice.* But like freedom, diversity can devour itself, and choice will disappear.

Beware of those who teach a diversity in which everybody, every philosophy, and all behavior must be accepted everywhere with standards adjusted to accommodate and to please everyone. They are really arguing for their own brand of conformity.

For example, if we change the standards at Church schools, and there are some who really press for that so that we conform more to the world, we lose the very idea of an education rooted in faith in the restored gospel. Then there will be no choice, and diversity will have eaten itself up.

The hidden trap connected with diversity is that a misunderstanding of it can cause you to accept what *is* and lose sight of what *ought to be.*

We must and will maintain high standards in the Church in the name of choice and diversity. We have the right to create environments in our Church schools, in our institutes of religion, and individually in our minds, in our homes, and in the Church at large to create a Zion.

The Challenge of Learning

Those of you who attend Church schools are under the influence of teachers whose dedication and commitment will be a blessing to you for as long as you live. Their purpose is to open your mind to the secular and spiritual truths that will ensure a happy life.

Whether they teach secular subjects or classes in religion, their teaching and their behavior is a worthy example to follow. They enjoy the full trust of the Brethren, and their service deserves the gratitude of all members in the Church.

Reluctantly, I alert you to the possibility that among them are one or two who deliberately inject students with diseased ideas. The test depends on whether they are teaching *about* false standards or theories or philosophies or whether they are *advocates* of them. You must discern whether you are being taught *about* an ideology or proselyted to it.

A teacher (and I remind you they are few) who advocates false philosophies or lower standards of conduct, supposing to prepare students for the realities of life, is as foolish as a woman I learned about in a junior high health class.

Upon learning that the neighbor children had chicken pox, she sent her children to play with them so that she could get that out of the way. When one of the neighbor children died, she learned to her horror that it was small pox, not chicken pox, to which she had exposed her children.

You probably will not meet such a teacher in Church schools. But should that happen, do not be intimidated by one who advocates philosophies or behavior that are in opposition to the standards set by the Lord and entrusted to His servants—those who have established, who finance, and who are responsible to administer our schools, our institutes of religion.

Students in our schools have both the right and the responsibility to challenge such teachings. That may be part of your test. Students or teachers who feel uncomfortable in our environment are free to choose another, but they are not free to substitute their own ideals or standards of behavior for those expected in an institution supported by the tithes and offerings of the Saints.

State Schools

You who are in state colleges have a different challenge. For the most part, your professors will be men and women of integrity, and you can trust them. But here too there are those few who do not deserve your trust. This may well be your greatest test in school. The tests on paper by comparison are only incidental.

Remember what Paul told young Timothy: "Neglect not the gift that is in thee" (1 Timothy 4:14).

There are angels to attend you. "Angels," the scriptures tell us, "speak by the power of the Holy Ghost" (2 Nephi 32:3). You received the Holy Ghost as a gift at the time of your confirmation as a member of the Church.

You will be guided as to how to meet these challenges and become stronger for having met them.

Flight Training

At the end of advanced flight training during World War II, it was customary for each instructor pilot at our base to invite his cadets to a dinner the week before graduation. Final decisions on graduation were yet to be made, and we were all very sensitive that it was by the word of our instructor that we would get our commission as an officer and those coveted silver wings.

Our instructor took us to a noisy roadhouse near the airbase in Marfa, Texas. He said, "The drinks are on me! Drink up and enjoy yourselves!" I managed to get by on soft drinks until the cadet sitting next to me blurted out, "Captain Goff, do you know what Packer is doing?" I gave him a jab with my elbow and whispered to him something that had to do with his not living very long. And before long no one seemed to be paying much attention to *anything,* and I survived the challenge.

I suppose I handled that as best I could. Looking back on it, I think there would have been a much better way. I could have, and I should have, told my instructor beforehand of my convictions, that my faith prohibited me from drinking liquor. If I had done so, surely I could have avoided that crisis.

If your professor is reasonable, you might tell him that your church encourages you to learn about all things, but your faith gives you reasons for not accepting every theory or philosophy that anyone believes to be true.

Sometimes even that may not be advisable. Just remember, you are not alone. You have the spirit of inspiration to guide you in your studies, in your tests, and in your contacts in the world. Have courage and remember who you are and that you are on stage in Act II of the great plan of redemption. You can know by the Spirit those teachers you can safely trust. A knowledge of the plan of happiness can help you through the difficult times and to face problems you otherwise could not endure.

For example, some years ago a president of a student stake asked if I would counsel with a young couple. The stalwart young man and his lovely wife had recently been told, with some finality, that they would never have children of their own. They were heartbroken as they sobbed out their disappointment. What they wanted most in life, what they had been taught and knew was an obligation and a privilege beyond price (part of the plan), they now were to be denied. Why? Why? Why?

I consoled them as best I could and offered comfort that really was insufficient to quiet the pain they felt. As they were leaving the office, I called them back and said, "You are a very fortunate and very blessed young couple."

They were startled, and the young man asked why I would say such a thing as that. Did I not understand what they had told me? Why would I say they were fortunate and blessed when they were to be denied the thing they wanted most, children of their own.

I answered, "Because you *want* them. In the eternal scheme of things, that will be of inestimable and eternal value." The Lord has said that He "will judge all men according to their works, according to the desire of their hearts" (D&C 137:9). Many people now do not want children or want few of them or consider them a burden rather than a blessing. They were a very blessed young couple.

When you understand the plan, you can cope with challenges in life that otherwise would be unbearable.

Now, when I speak of the law and of rules, I always get a letter or two pointing out a variation or an exception. There is an old saying that the exception proves the rule. That's a true statement.

You be careful that you don't look for exceptions as an excuse to avoid keeping the rules, and don't trust those who do. If something has to be labeled an exception, really it does prove the rule.

The Broken Carving

Now, if you suppose some of you, because of mistakes you have already made, have lost your future, let me, in conclusion, teach you this—one more inoculation:

For a number of years I found relaxation in carving and painting songbirds—at times spending a full year on a single carving. That suggests how much time I had now and again. Once I had a newly finished carving on the back seat of a car driven by Elder A. Theodore Tuttle. He hit the brakes suddenly, and the carving was thrown to the floor and damaged.

Elder Tuttle felt terrible, supposing he had ruined a year's work. When I waved aside his apologies, he said, "You sure don't seem to be upset about it." To reassure him, I said, "Don't worry. I made it; I can fix it." Actually it had been broken and fixed many times while I was working on it.

Later, Brother Tuttle likened that experience to individuals whose lives were broken or badly damaged, supposedly ruined with no hope of repair, who did not know that there is a Maker, a Creator, who can fix any of His creations no matter how hopelessly broken they seem to be.

God bless you precious youth of the Church, you young adults all over the world. Recently we met with your counterparts in Seoul, Korea, and the week before in Tokyo, Japan—young, hopeful Latter-day Saints who are the strength of the kingdom of God upon the earth. God bless you as you find your way. Remember, there is no final curtain on the third act of this great drama. It goes on eternally.

I bear witness that Jesus is the Christ, the Son of God, that the gospel of Jesus Christ is true, that you as young members of the Church may look forward to a wonderful life of challenges and happiness and responsibility. It is a wonderful time to live and to be young. I envy you. As I said in the beginning, you are young and I am not. And yet in the eternal scheme of things, I am just as young as you are. Maybe I'm a little closer to the final curtain in Act II, but I know, for I have seen a little behind the curtain into Act III, and bear personal witness that the gospel is true, and I bear witness of Jesus Christ.

In closing, I invoke a blessing upon you, you young men and young women who I hope are looking for a companion, you newly married men and women starting a family—looking forward to the adventure in life—may the power of the Lord watch over you and His Spirit attend you. The Holy Ghost will bless you with a testimony.

Fear is the antithesis of faith. In this Church we do not fear. I have been sitting in the councils of the Brethren now for some thirty-four years or so. I have seen disappointment, shock, and concern. Never once, for one second, have I ever seen any fear. And you should not.

May He bless you as you find your way. I am sure He will. I bear that witness to you and invoke that blessing upon you.

23

TEACH THE CHILDREN

It occurred to me recently that in three weeks I will reach my seventy-fifth birthday and move into what I choose to call *upper middle age.*

I have been a teacher for more than fifty years. And I have learned this from experience: Life will teach us some things we didn't think we wanted to know. These hard lessons can be the most valuable ones.

I learned something else about learning on my way to *upper middle age.* Consider this conversation between a doctor and a patient:

Doctor: "How can I help you? What seems to be your problem?"

Patient: "It is my memory, doctor. I read something, and I can't remember it. I can't remember why I came into a room. I can't remember where I put things."

Doctor: "Well, tell me, how long has this condition been bothering you?"

Patient: "How long has what condition been bothering me?"

From an address given at a Brigham Young University Education Week devotional, August 17, 1999; see *Ensign*, February 2000, 10–17.

Now, if that amused you, you are either under sixty or you are laughing at yourself.

Teaching Children While They're Young

When you grow older, you cannot learn or memorize or study like you could when you were young. Could that be why the prophet Alma counseled, "Learn wisdom in thy youth; yea, learn in thy youth to keep the commandments of God" (Alma 37:35)?

It is increasingly difficult for me to memorize scriptures and lines of poetry. In my youth I could repeat something a time or two and remember it. If I said it over many times, particularly if I wrote it down, it was quite permanently recorded in my mind.

Youth is the time for easy learning. That is why the teachers of children and youth have been such a concern for the leaders of the Church from the very beginning.

It is consummately important to teach the gospel and life's lessons to children and youth.

The Lord places the first responsibility upon parents and warns them: "Inasmuch as parents have children in Zion, . . . that teach them not to understand the doctrine of repentance, faith in Christ the Son of the living God, and of baptism and the gift of the Holy Ghost by the laying on of the hands, when eight years old, the sin be upon the heads of the parents" (D&C 68:25).

It is the basic purpose of this Church to teach the youth: first in the home and then in church.

Storing Up Knowledge

Another thing I have learned has to do with remembering what we learned when we were young. Knowledge stored in young minds may wait many years for the moment when it might be needed.

Let me illustrate. I am very concerned about the tendency of members to disregard the counsel of the bishop or, at the other extreme, to become overdependent upon him. And so I decided to speak in general conference about the bishop.

I prayerfully prepared, and there came to mind a conversation from fifty years past. It served my need as a teacher—served it perfectly. I quote now that conversation, just as I did in general conference:

"Years ago I served on a stake high council with Emery Wight. For 10 years Emery had served as bishop of rural Harper Ward. His wife, Lucille, became our stake Relief Society president.

"Lucille told me that one spring morning a neighbor called at her door and asked for Emery. She told him that he was out plowing. The neighbor then spoke with great concern. Earlier that morning he had passed the field and noticed Emery's team of horses standing in a half-finished furrow with the reins draped over the plow. Emery was nowhere in sight. The neighbor thought nothing of it until much later when he passed the field again, and the team had not moved. He climbed the fence and crossed the field to the horses. Emery was nowhere to be found. The neighbor hurried to the house to check with Lucille.

"Lucille calmly replied, 'Oh, don't be alarmed. No doubt someone is in trouble and came to get the bishop.'

"The image of that team of horses standing for hours in the field symbolizes the dedication of the bishops in the Church and of the counselors who stand by their side. Every bishop and every counselor, figuratively speaking, leaves his team standing in an unfinished furrow when someone needs help" ("The Bishop and His Counselors," *Ensign,* May 1999, 57).

I had never before used that experience in a talk—never thought of it.

I wanted to fix it in my mind before speaking of it in conference, so I located a daughter of Emery Wight. She agreed to meet me at their old home and show me the field her father would have been plowing that day.

One of my sons took me there early one Sunday morning. He took a number of pictures. It was a beautiful spring morning. The field was newly plowed, just as it had been those many years before. Seagulls were feeding in the newly turned soil.

That quickened memory, remembering that conversation, is not uncommon to me. It reaffirms the truth of the scripture—one, incidentally, I memorized in my youth—"Neither take ye thought beforehand what ye shall say; but treasure up in your minds continually the words of life, and it shall be given you in the very hour that portion that shall be meted unto every man" (D&C 84:85).

There follows a promise to those who treasure up knowledge: "Whoso receiveth you, there I will be also, for I will go before your face. I will be on your right hand and on your left, and my Spirit shall be in your hearts, and mine angels round about you, to bear you up" (D&C 84:88).

It was a good lesson for me, but my lesson did not end there.

I had done some painting and wood carving in my youth. I was largely self-taught. While the children were growing up, my time was devoted to teaching them things I had learned about life and about carving and painting when I was a boy.

After they were grown, I took up wood carving as a means of relaxation. I carved birds and spent many hours on a carving. When asked, "How many hours did it take you to carve this?" I always answered, "I don't know. If I found out, I would quit." During those hours working with my hands, I pondered on the marvels of creation, and inspiration would flow. As I carved wood, I carved out talks.

Carving was restful to me. Sometimes when I got a little stressed and cranky, my wife would say, "Well, you had better start another carving."

I suppose if my *upper middle age* memory sharpened itself a bit, I could point to one of those carvings and tell which talk it represents. I learned that in those quiet moments I could do two things at once.

Reaping a Harvest from Teaching

I am no longer able to do those carvings. That work is too delicate for me with trifocals and finger joints that now stiffen a bit from childhood polio. Besides, the increasing pressure of my calling limits the time I can devote both to carving and to preparing talks. The ability to carve now is largely lost to me but not to our children. We taught them when they were young.

The image of that team standing in the field stayed with me. I thought that perhaps I could do a painting of the bishop's team standing in the field with the reins draped over the plow.

I hesitated because it had been nine years since I had painted a picture. Two friends with unusual talent and inspiration offered to help me paint the bishop's team, and July gave a respite from travel, so I began.

I learned much from those two friends, and in a real way they are in my painting. But I received more help from my two sons. One son took those pictures of the plowed field, for I try always to be very accurate when depicting something in *wood* or on *canvas* or with *words*.

The other son decided to do a sculpture of the bishop's team to be cast in bronze as a companion to my painting. We spent many rewarding hours helping one another.

He took from our barn a couple of old harnesses which have hung essentially untouched for more than fifty years. He dusted them off and took them home. He draped one harness over a very patient riding horse. It stood quietly as he arranged the harness in proper order and made detailed sketches of it.

His neighbor had collected some old plows. Among them was a plow of proper vintage, which he also sketched.

And so there came back that which we had given those sons in their youth. As with our other children, they have improved on that which we as parents taught them when they were very young. That is another lesson. I could draw back from our children something they had learned when they were young. And if our days are prolonged upon the earth, there comes a second harvest—our grandchildren—and perhaps a third.

Reawakening Dormant Talents

I relearned something else. Once before I had painted a picture inspired by comments that I heard when I was a boy. It depicted the Willard Peaks. I had heard the older folks refer to them as *The Presidency.* These three gigantic, solid peaks standing against the sky typified the leaders of the Church.

That was nine years ago. My son had taken me to Willard, Utah, and photographed the peaks. We went back a second time when there would be more shadow and contrast. After those years I had to awaken that which I had let go dormant. At first it was a terrible struggle. I threatened to quit several times. One of my friends urged me on by saying, "Go ahead! There's always plenty of room at the bottom."

I did not quit, simply because my wife would not give me permission to do so. I am glad I didn't now. Perhaps, now that I am into it again, I'll do another painting sometime—who knows?

I suppose trying to get back into painting is not unlike someone who has been inactive in the Church for many years and decides to return to the fold. There is that period of struggle in getting the feel for what has lain dormant but is not really lost. And it helps to have a friend or two.

That is another principle of learning—drawing lessons from ordinary experience in life. That painting of *The Bishop's Team* will soon be finished. My son's sculpture is at the foundry being cast in bronze.

His sculpture, incidentally, is much better than my painting. That is as it should be. His young fingers and mind respond more readily than mine do.

As we move to *upper middle age,* we learn that old bones don't bend easily, older joints don't move so quickly. It is not easy to tie your shoes once you move past your middle sixties—then they lower the floors.

There comes that lesson again: "Learn wisdom in thy youth; yea, learn in thy youth to keep the commandments of God" (Alma 37:35).

"The glory of God is intelligence, or, in other words, light and truth" (D&C 93:36).

"I have commanded you to bring up your children in light and truth" (D&C 93:40).

The supernal gift of the Holy Ghost is conferred upon our children when they are only eight years of age.

"The Comforter, which is the Holy Ghost, whom the Father will send in my name, he shall *teach* you *all* things, and bring *all* things to your *remembrance*, whatsoever I have said unto you" (John 14:26; italics added).

Notice the words *teach* and *remembrance.* Teaching children brings its own reward. Have you not yet learned that when you teach you learn more from teaching than do your children from learning?

Drawing on Spiritual Memories

There is a difference between acquiring temporal knowledge and acquiring spiritual knowledge. Students learn that on test day. It is awfully hard to remember something you didn't learn in the first place.

That is true of temporal knowledge, but spiritually we can draw on a memory that goes back beyond birth. We may develop a sensitivity to things that were not understood when we were younger.

The poet Wordsworth felt something about premortal life when he wrote:

> *Our birth is but a sleep and a forgetting:*
> *The Soul that rises with us, our life's Star,*
> *Hath had elsewhere its setting,*
> *And cometh from afar:*

Not in entire forgetfulness,
And not in utter nakedness,
But trailing clouds of glory do we come
From God, who is our home.

(From "Ode: Intimations of Immortality from Recollections of Early Childhood," in *The Oxford Book of English Verse: 1250–1900,* ed. Arthur Quiller-Couch [1939], 638)

I drew those lines from my memory, where I stored them during an English class in my college days.

The most important lessons come from ordinary events in life.

Some wait for compelling spiritual experiences to confirm their testimony. It doesn't work that way. It is the quiet promptings and impressions of ordinary things that give us the assurance of our identity as children of God. We live far below our privileges when we seek after signs and look "beyond the mark" (Jacob 4:14) for marvelous events.

We are children of God, for we lived with Him in the premortal existence. From time to time that curtain is parted. There comes to us the intimation of who we are and of our place in the eternal scheme of things. Call that memory or spiritual insight, it is one of those testimonies that the gospel of Jesus Christ is true. Such revelations come when we are teaching.

I once heard President Marion G. Romney (1897–1988) say, "I always know when I am speaking under the influence of the Holy Ghost because I always learn something from what I have said."

The Lord told the elders:

"Ye are not sent forth to be taught, but to teach the children of men the things which I have put into your hands by the power of my Spirit;

"And ye are to be taught from on high. Sanctify yourselves and ye shall be endowed with power, that ye may give even as I have spoken" (D&C 43:15–16).

Even when the harvest of converts is meager for missionaries, a spiritual power comes to them and to the Church because they learn through their teaching.

The president of a quorum of deacons is to sit in council and teach his fellow deacons (see D&C 107:85). The president of a quorum of elders is to teach the members of his quorum according to the covenants (see D&C 107:89).

Paul told Timothy, "The things that thou hast heard of me among many witnesses, the same commit thou to faithful men, who shall be able to teach others also" (2 Timothy 2:2).

He explained in nine words how teaching becomes its own reward:

"Thou therefore which teachest another, teachest thou not thyself? thou that preachest a man should not steal, dost thou steal?

"Thou that sayest a man should not commit adultery, dost thou commit adultery?" (Romans 2:21–22; italics added).

Being a Willing Learner

The scriptures contain many references revealing how "hard" to bear the teachings of the prophets and apostles were for the Israelites and for the Nephites (see John 6:60; 1 Nephi 16:2; 2 Nephi 9:40; Helaman 14:10). It is so easy to resist the teaching and resent the teacher. That has been the lot of the prophets and apostles from the beginning.

One of the Beatitudes teaches that "blessed are ye, when men shall revile you, and persecute you, and shall say all manner of evil against you falsely, for my sake.

"Rejoice, and be exceeding glad: for great is your reward in heaven: for so persecuted they the prophets which were before you" (Matthew 5:11–12; see also Luke 21:12; John 15:20, 3 Nephi 12:12).

I sometimes receive letters of apology, which say something like the following: "I could not understand why you felt the need to make me feel so uncomfortable and so guilty." Then, out of their struggle, there emerges an insight, an inspiration, an understanding of causes and effects. Finally they come to see and understand why the gospel is as it is.

I mention one among several subjects. A sister may finally come to see why we stress the importance of mothers staying at home with their children. She understands that no service equals the exalting refinement which comes through unselfish motherhood. Nor does she need to forgo intellectual or cultural or social refinement. Those things are fitted in—in proper time—for they attend the everlasting virtue which comes from teaching children.

No teaching is equal, more spiritually rewarding, or more exalting than that of a mother teaching her children. A mother may feel inadequate in scripture scholarship because she is occupied in teaching her family. She will not receive a lesser reward.

President Grant Bangerter was having a doctrinal conversation with President Joseph Fielding Smith, who was touring his mission in Brazil. Sister Bangerter listened and finally said, "President Smith, I have been raising children and haven't had time to become a scriptorian like he is. Will I get to the celestial kingdom with Grant?"

President Smith pondered soberly for a moment and then said, "Well, perhaps if you bake him a pie."

A man will be hard pressed to equal that measure of spiritual refinement that accrues naturally to his wife as she teaches their children. And if he understands the gospel at all, he knows that he cannot be exalted without her (see D&C 131:1–4; 132:19–21). His best hope is to lead out as an attentive, responsible partner in teaching their children.

Blessings to Teachers

Now, consider this promise: "Teach ye diligently and my grace shall attend *you* [the teacher], that you [the teacher, the mother, the father] may be instructed more perfectly in theory, in principle, in doctrine, in the law of the gospel, in all things that pertain unto the kingdom of

God, that are expedient for you [the mother, the father] to understand" (D&C 88:78; italics added).

Notice the promise is to the teacher rather than to the student.

"Teach ye diligently and my grace shall attend you [who teach your children or Primary, Sunday School, Young Women and Men, priesthood, seminary, Relief Society]," that you may come to know:

"Of things both in heaven and in the earth, and under the earth; things which have been, things which are, things which must shortly come to pass; things which are at home, things which are abroad; the wars and the perplexities of the nations, and the judgments which are on the land; and a knowledge also of countries and of kingdoms—

"That ye [who teach] may be prepared in all things when I shall send you again to magnify the calling whereunto I have called you, and the mission with which I have commissioned you" (D&C 88:79–80).

Paul prophesied to young Timothy "that in the last days perilous times shall come" (2 Timothy 3:1). He said, "Evil men and seducers shall wax worse and worse, deceiving, and being deceived" (2 Timothy 3:13).

But we can still be safe. Our safety is in teaching the children: "Train up a child in the way he should go: and when he is old, he will not depart from it" (Proverbs 22:6).

Paul counseled Timothy: "Continue thou in the things which thou hast learned and hast been assured of, knowing of whom thou hast learned them;

"And that from a *child* thou hast *known the holy scriptures,* which are able to make thee wise unto salvation through faith which is in Christ Jesus" (2 Timothy 3:14–15; italics added).

This is the Church of Jesus Christ. It is His Church. He is our Exemplar, our Redeemer. We are commanded to be "even as he is" (1 John 3:7).

He was a teacher of children. He commanded His disciples at Jerusalem to "suffer little children, and forbid them not, to come unto me: for of such is the kingdom of heaven" (Matthew 19:14).

In the account of the Savior's ministry among the Nephites, we can see deeper into His soul perhaps than at any other place:

"And it came to pass that he commanded that their little children should be brought.

"So they brought their little children and set them down upon the ground round about him, and Jesus stood in the midst; and the multitude gave way till they had all been brought unto him. . . .

" . . . He wept, and the multitude bare record of it, and he took their little children, one by one, and blessed them, and prayed unto the Father for them.

"And when he had done this he wept again;

"And he spake unto the multitude, and said unto them: Behold your little ones.

"And as they looked to behold they cast their eyes towards heaven, and they saw the heavens open, and they saw angels descending out of heaven as it were in the midst of fire; and they came down and encircled those little ones about, and they were encircled about with fire; and the angels did minister unto them.

"And the multitude did see and hear and bear record; and they know that their record is true for they all of them did see and hear" (3 Nephi 17:11–12, 21–25).

PART SIX

LESSONS FROM OUR LEADERS

24

COVENANTS

In the last session of the October 1986 general conference, Elder A. Theodore Tuttle gave a touching and inspiring sermon on faith. He spoke from his heart, with scriptures in hand, without a prepared text. When he had concluded, President Gordon B. Hinckley, who conducted that session, said: "I should perhaps be guilty of an indiscretion, but I think I will risk it and say that Brother Tuttle has been seriously ill and he needs our faith, the faith of which he has spoken. It will be appreciated if those who have listened to him across the Church would plead with our Father in Heaven, in the kind of faith which he has described, in his behalf" (Conference Report, October 1986, 93).

President Ezra Taft Benson, who was the concluding speaker, endorsed what President Hinckley had said and appealed himself for fasting and prayers of faith for the recovery of Brother Tuttle.

But Brother Tuttle did not recover. He died seven weeks later.

Now, lest there be one whose faith was shaken, believing prayers

---

From an address given at general conference, April 4, 1987; see *Ensign*, May 1987, 22–24.

were not answered, or lest there be one who is puzzled that the prophet himself could plead for the entire Church to fast and pray for Brother Tuttle to live and yet he died, I will tell you of an experience.

I had intended to tell this at his funeral, but my feelings were too tender that day to speak of it.

One Sunday when Brother Tuttle was at home, confined mostly to his bed, I spent a few hours with him while Marné and the family went to church.

He was deeply moved by the outpouring of love from across the world. Each letter extended prayers of faith for his recovery. Many of the messages came from South America, where the Tuttle family had labored for so many years.

That day we reviewed his life, beginning with his birth in Manti, Utah, to an ordinary Latter-day Saint couple. We talked of his father, whom I knew, and of his mother, a faithful temple worker.

He talked of his mission, his college days, his marriage to Marné Whitaker, and his heroic service in the marines.

Then we relived our days teaching seminary in Brigham City and supervising the seminaries and institutes of religion.

He talked of his seven faithful children and the flock of grandchildren whom he always described as "the best kids in the world."

He spoke of his call to the First Quorum of the Seventy and the assignments that followed. Soon the Tuttle family was called to South America. They were hardly settled back home when the Brethren interviewed him about returning.

Others could say, "Of course, if you should *call* us, we would go." But not him, nor Marné, for they had made covenants. Without complaint, his wife and family followed him back time after time for a total of seven years.

No matter that he had never recovered from serious physical troubles which began on his first assignment there. That day Brother

Tuttle spoke tenderly of the humble people of Latin America. They who have so little have greatly blessed his life.

He insisted that he did not deserve more blessings, nor did he need them. Others needed them more. And then he told me this: "I talked to the Lord about those prayers for my recovery. I asked if the blessings were mine to do with as I pleased. If that could be so, I told the Lord that I wanted him to take them back from me and give them to those who needed them more."

He said, "I begged the Lord to take back those blessings and give them to others."

Brother Tuttle wanted those blessings from our prayers for those struggling souls whom most of us hardly remember, but whom he could not forget.

The scriptures teach that "the effectual fervent prayer of a righteous man availeth much" (James 5:16).

Can you not believe that the Lord may have favored the pleadings of this saintly man above our own appeal for his recovery?

We do not know all things, but is it wrong to suppose that our prayers were not in vain at all? Who among us would dare to say that humble folk here and there across the continent of South America will not receive unexpected blessings passed on to them from this man who was without guile?

May not lofty purposes such as this be worked out in our lives if we are submissive?

Now, I know that skeptics may ridicule such things. But I, for one, am content to believe that our prayers were accepted and recorded and redirected to those whose hands hang down in despair, just as Brother Tuttle had requested.

In any case, ought we not to conclude all our prayers with "Let thy will, O Lord, be done"?

During his last weeks he was always pleasant, invariably comforting those who came to comfort him. I was present when he called his doctors to his bedside and thanked each one for the care he had received.

He was determined to live through Thanksgiving Day lest his passing cast a shadow of sorrow upon his family on that holiday in future years. That evening he saw each of his children, called those who were away, expressed his love and blessings, and bade them farewell. It was very late when they reached Clarie, who lives in Alaska, but his parting must be delayed until that was done.

Early the next morning, without resistance, with a spirit of quiet anticipation, he slipped away. At that moment, there came into that room a spirit of peace which surpasseth understanding.

Marné had been before, was then, and has been since, a perfect example of serenity and acceptance.

Now, to draw a lesson from this experience.

Brother Tuttle served twenty-eight years as a General Authority. He traveled the world. He supervised the work in Europe for a time. But with all the places he would go and all of the things he was to do, he repeatedly said that the crowning experience of his ministry was his service as president of the Provo Temple with his beloved Marné at his side.

Few know the demanding schedule of a temple president. The day may begin at three in the morning and end only too close to that same hour.

It was not that he was presiding *over* the temple but that the calling allowed him to be *in* the temple. He would have been quite content to serve under another. His feelings about that assignment were not due so much to his understanding of what a *call* is, as it was his understanding of what a *covenant* is.

A covenant is a sacred promise, as used in the scriptures, a solemn, enduring promise between God and man. The fulness of the gospel itself is defined as the new and everlasting covenant (see D&C 22:1; 66:2).

Several years ago I installed a stake president in England. He had an unusual sense of direction. He was like a mariner with a sextant who took his bearings from the stars. I met with him each time he came to conference and was impressed that he kept himself and his stake on course.

Fortunately for me, when it was time for his release, I was assigned to reorganize the stake. It was then that I discovered what that sextant was and how he adjusted it to check his position and get a bearing for himself and for his members.

He accepted his release and said, "I was happy to accept the call to serve as stake president, and I am equally happy to accept my release. I did not serve just because I was under *call*. I served because I am under *covenant*. And I can keep my covenants quite as well as a home teacher as I can serving as stake president."

This president understood the word *covenant*.

While he was neither a scriptorian nor a gospel scholar, he somehow had learned that exaltation is achieved by keeping covenants, not by holding high position.

The mariner gets his bearing from light coming from celestial bodies—the sun by day, the stars by night. That stake president did not need a mariner's sextant to set his course. In his mind there was a sextant infinitely more refined and precise than any mariner's instrument.

The spiritual sextant, which each of us has, also functions on the principle of light from celestial sources. Set that sextant in your mind to the word *covenant* or the word *ordinance*. The light will come through. Then you can fix your position and set a true course in life.

No matter what citizenship or race, whether male or female, no matter what occupation, no matter your education, regardless of the generation in which one lives, life is a homeward journey for all of us, back to the presence of God in His celestial kingdom.

Ordinances and covenants become our credentials for admission into His presence. To worthily receive them is the quest of a lifetime; to keep them thereafter is the challenge of mortality.

Once we have received them for ourselves and for our families, we are obligated to provide these ordinances vicariously for our kindred dead, indeed for the whole human family.

Now, there are those who scoff at the idea of vicarious ordinances performed for the salvation of souls. They think it all to be very strange.

No thinking Christian should be surprised at such a doctrine. Was not the sacrifice of Christ a vicarious offering for and in behalf of all mankind? The very Atonement was wrought vicariously.

The Lord did for us what we could not do for ourselves. Is it not Christlike for us to perform in the temples ordinances for and in behalf of those who cannot do them for themselves?

Genealogies, or family histories, as I prefer to call them, are an indispensable part of temple work. Temples are nourished with names. Without genealogies, ordinances could be performed only for the living. Searching out the names of our kindred dead is a duty of consummate importance. There is a spirit which accompanies this work very similar to that which attends us in the temple itself.

Missionaries and those with small children may not be able to devote much time to this work at present, but you can keep the spirit of it. You can talk to the old folks and record what they say, keep family records, attend the temple.

There is the tendency on the part of some to regard genealogy work as a tedious, onerous burden. And they are quite content to leave it to the aged or to others "who have an interest in such things."

Be careful! It may well be that those who have that interest in such things have chosen the better part. And I would say to you, if you are called to other service or do not have an interest in genealogy, do not belittle or stand in the way of those who do. Give them every encouragement; contribute what you can.

The Prophet Joseph Smith said: "The doctrine or sealing power of Elijah is as follows:—If you have power to seal on earth and in heaven, then we should be wise. The first thing you do, go and seal on earth your sons and daughters unto yourself, and yourself unto your fathers in eternal glory" (*Teachings of the Prophet Joseph Smith,* sel. Joseph Fielding Smith [1976], 340).

The Spirit of Elijah of which the prophets have spoken is very real and accompanies those who seek for the records of their kindred dead.

The more I have to do with genealogical work, the more difficulty I have with that word *dead.* I know of no adequate substitute. I suppose *departed* would suit me as well as any. I have had too many sacred experiences, of the kind of which we never speak lightly, to feel that the word *dead* describes those who have gone beyond the veil.

Temple and genealogy work are visible testimonies of our belief in the Resurrection and Atonement of the Lord Jesus Christ. Should we doubt that we live again beyond the veil, what reason would we have to do the things we are doing?

This work is our witness of the redemptive power of the sacrifice of the Lord Jesus Christ.

Now, what of Brother Tuttle or of his family? I remind you that it is a veil, not a wall, that separates us from the spirit world. He kept his covenants. Veils can become thin, even parted. We are not left to do this work alone.

They who have preceded us in this work and our forebears there, on occasion, are very close to us. I have a testimony of this work; it is a supernal work in the Church. I am a witness that those who go beyond the veil yet live and minister here, to the end that this work might be completed.

25

SPENCER W. KIMBALL:
NO ORDINARY MAN

President Kimball once said: "What mother, looking down with tenderness upon her chubby infant does not envision her child as the President of the Church or the leader of her nation! As he is nestled in her arms, she sees him a statesman, a leader, a prophet. Some dreams do come true! One mother gives us a Shakespeare, another a Michelangelo, and another an Abraham Lincoln, and still another a Joseph Smith!

"When theologians are reeling and stumbling, when lips are pretending and hearts are wandering, and people are 'running to and fro, seeking the word of the Lord and cannot find it'—when clouds of error need dissipating and spiritual darkness needs penetrating and heavens need opening, a little infant is born" (Conference Report, April 1960, 84).

And so came Spencer Woolley Kimball. The Lord had managed those humble beginnings. He was not just preparing a businessman, nor a civic leader, nor a speaker, nor a poet, nor a musician, nor a

From *Ensign*, March 1974, 2–13.

teacher—though he would be all of these. He was preparing a father, a patriarch for his family, an apostle and prophet, and a president for His church.

There were testings along the way. Examinations in courage and patience that few would have passed. As a little lad he suffered a facial paralysis that yielded only to the administrations of the priesthood. On one occasion he nearly drowned but was revived.

When he was eleven years old, his mother, who was expecting the twelfth child, was not doing well and was taken by his father to Salt Lake City, where better medical attention was available.

One day the word came to the little school that the Kimball children were wanted at home. Little Spencer came running from his classroom to meet his brothers and sisters in the hall. They all raced home, there to find Bishop Moody. He gathered them all into his arms and then with a voice full of love and anguish said, "Your mama has died." (Later would come a loving stepmother.)

When he was thirteen, as a motherless boy, he contracted typhoid and for weeks lay at the point of death. Smallpox followed; and there were other trials and there was other suffering, some known to a few, and some known to none but him.

After his call to the Twelve, he suffered a series of heart attacks. The doctors said that he must rest. He wanted to be with his beloved Indians. Brother Golden R. Buchanan took him to the camp of Brother and Sister Polacca, high in the pines of Arizona, and there he stayed during the weeks until his heart mended and his strength returned.

One morning he was missing from camp. When he did not return for breakfast, Brother Polacca and other Indian friends began to search. They found him several miles from camp, sitting beneath a large pine tree with his Bible open to the last chapter of the Gospel of John. In answer to their worried looks, he said, "Six years ago today I was called to be an Apostle of the Lord Jesus Christ. And I just wanted to spend the day with Him whose witness I am."

His heart problems recurred but did not slow him down for long. In 1957 throat problems developed, to be diagnosed as cancer of the throat and of the vocal cords. This, perhaps, was to be his Gethsemane.

He went east for the operation. Elder Harold B. Lee was there. As he was prepared for surgery, he agonized over the ominous possibilities, telling the Lord that he did not see how he could live without a voice, for his voice to preach and to speak was his ministry.

"This is no ordinary man you're operating on," Elder Lee told the surgeon. From the blessings and the prayers, an operation a bit less radical than the doctor recommended was performed.

There was a long period of recuperation and preparation. The voice was all but gone, but a new one took its place. A quiet, persuasive, mellow voice, an acquired voice, an appealing voice, a voice that is loved by the Latter-day Saints.

In the intervening time he could work. During interviews he tapped out on the typewriter answers to questions and spent his time at the office.

Then came the test. Could he speak? Could he preach?

He went back home for his maiden speech. He went back to *the* valley. Anyone close to him knows it is not *a* valley, it is *the* valley. There, in a conference of the St. Joseph Stake, accompanied by his beloved associate from Arizona, Elder Delbert L. Stapley, he stood at the pulpit.

"I have come back here," he said, "to be among my own people. In this valley I presided as stake president." Perhaps he thought that should he fail, here he would be among those who loved him most and would understand.

There was a great outpouring of love. The tension of this dramatic moment was broken when he continued: "I must tell you what has happened to me. I went away to the East, and while there I fell among cutthroats." After that it didn't matter what he said. Elder Kimball was back!

On another occasion while going to a conference in Arizona, his car slid off an icy dugway in the Kaibab Forest, rolled down the mountainside over large boulders, and landed on a wood road below. The wood road providentially provided immediate access. Sister Kimball was seriously injured and was taken to the hospital in Kanab. After seeing to her needs, and with her urging, Elder Kimball boarded a bus to attend the conference.

When throat problems recurred, he underwent treatment, almost between appointments in his office.

He had Bell's palsy for several weeks with the drooping muscles in his face.

Two years ago his doctors advised heart surgery to correct the early damage to his heart. His associates remember the agony of his decision. What would the outcome be? The doctors shook their heads, for there were no statistics on seventy-seven-year-old men undergoing open heart surgery for such major repair.

But again, this was no ordinary man the doctors were operating on, and the surgeon sought a blessing under the hands of President Harold B. Lee. "A composite of two procedures at once made it one of the most risky and complex operations ever done," said his surgeon.

There have been many more experiences, but these are representative of the obstacles and challenges he has overcome. In all of this there has been a remarkable patience and absence of complaint. He has kept his discouragement to himself and would not miss an appointment.

Those closely associated with him have seen that these problems have had some effect on his working habits, best characterized by a quote from one of the Twelve who said, "Yes, President Kimball isn't himself. He's cut down from eighteen to seventeen-and-a-half hours of work each day."

Happily his surgeon recently reported, "In a complete assessment of your general physical status, all of our findings were indicative of superb structure and function of your body. No individual has ever been called to preside over the Church with such thorough medical preparation and examination prior to his ordination. Your body is strong; your heart is better than it has been for years, and by all our finite ability to predict, you may consider this new assignment without undue anxiety about your health."

President Kimball himself is an experienced surgeon of sorts. Not a doctor of medicine, but a doctor of spiritual well-being. Many a moral cancer has been excised, many a blemish of character has been removed, many a spiritual illness of one kind or another has been cured through his efforts. Some on the verge of spiritual oblivion have been rescued by him. He has written a book—literally years in preparation—*The Miracle of Forgiveness.* Many have been protected by the counsel he has written. Countless others have been inspired to set their lives in order and have experienced that miracle.

There have been other trials too, greater far than those we have mentioned, too sacred to publish, but he has told his Brethren of the Twelve.

On two occasions, each time when he was on assignments to stake quarterly conference, and each time not related to problems incident to the conference, there was unleashed against him the very might of the adversary. He endured during those hours, not to be recorded here, something akin to what his grandfather had experienced when, as an Apostle of the Lord, he opened the work in England, something not unlike the Prophet Joseph experienced as he first knelt in the Grove.

These trials have made him humbly dependent upon the power of the Lord. To pray with Spencer W. Kimball is an experience!

All of the testing has not robbed him of his sense of humor. He is obviously a very happy man. When you travel with him there is many a chuckle. He makes those around him happy. His abundant humor is always in good taste.

On one occasion he was returning from Canada with one of his associates. The stewardess on the flight offered them all kinds of refreshments that are not proper for Latter-day Saints. After failing with coffee, tea, and alcoholic beverages, she asked, with some concern, "Isn't there anything I could get for you?"

"I would like some lemonade, if you have some," President Kimball replied.

"I'm sorry," she said, "We don't have any aboard."

She turned to go down the aisle and then no doubt remembered that lemon slices are often served with alcoholic beverages. She had some lemons aboard, for she turned and said, "But perhaps I could squeeze you a little."

President Kimball threw up his arms as a barrier and in an expression of mock concern replied, "Don't you touch me!"

He is happy and positive and always reassuring to be around. His handshake is hearty and warm and sincere, and he is ever alert to reach out to those who otherwise might be overlooked or ignored. Those who meet him for the first time are impressed at once with his courtesy.

A very visible characteristic of President Spencer W. Kimball is his penchant for hard work. When introducing the Welfare Program, the First Presidency declared, "Work is to be reenthroned as a ruling principle in the lives of our Church membership." He loves to work.

The blessing of work has been a principal characteristic of Spencer W. Kimball from the early days of his life. His father, a very meticulous and orderly man, wanted everything kept "just so." The fences should be painted, the yard should be kept in order. The harnesses well-oiled. The brass polished. This was not a well-to-do family but a family with a father busy as a stake president trying to support a large family. The cow and the vegetable garden were important.

The children were not without opportunity to play, but work was a governing principle in the household.

He said on one occasion, "There was never a new staple or a new strand of wire. It was always fix the fence with what there was, to put it together again somehow so that it would hold."

As a boy, as boys will, he wondered at the unending incessant toil necessary to make a living. And, as boys will, he thought how free he would feel when he got away from the farm and all the work involved.

Then came the day, years later, when as a young businessman, prospering perhaps a little, he was able to have a farm of his own. And he has told of the day that he walked out, took a handful of soil, and as it sifted through his fingers, reverently said to himself, "This is my land." Then he knew how much he loved the soil, what it meant to him in his life.

The family and the friends and associates of President Kimball know that he is never still. There has always been a restlessness about him to be getting things done. He is up early and works long hours and gets a little rest along the way. A time or two each day he will stretch out on the floor—perhaps in the bishop's office or the high council room if he is at a conference—and sleep for ten minutes. He bounces back with renewed energy to continue his thorough, detailed work.

I passed the Kimballs on the highway once, up near the Idaho border. They were heading north to conference. Sister Kimball was driving, with President Kimball in the back seat, his little typewriter in its accustomed place on his lap, papers on either side of him, for this was an opportunity to work, to do more to help others. This mobile office, as those who have traveled with him know, is characteristic of his dedication to work.

Where does he get the strength? Most of the sources are available to anyone—but one source, available to him alone, can be said in a word—Camilla.

Camilla Eyring went to teach at the academy in Thatcher, Arizona, and Spencer was attracted to the lovely girl from the colonies in Mexico. With her family she came out of Mexico in the exodus, fleeing before the armies of Pancho Villa. She had been encouraged by her parents to seek an education, and with limited means she had gone to Brigham Young University. She was attracted to the clean-cut, well-framed young man, with his alert sense of humor, with his sharp mind, with some music in his soul. There was what would have to be described as a whirlwind courtship. In a matter of weeks they knew they were right for one another. There began a companionship that will last through the eternities.

Sister Kimball is a remarkable woman. She is a woman of intelligence and culture and strength. But that is another story, an account that by all means ought to be written and printed and read.

The family is the center of all that is important to President Kimball. President and Sister Kimball have four children. They desired to have more, but that frail footpath of life over which spirits must cross into mortality is often beset with obstacles. It is sometimes very difficult and occasionally not possible to invite a spirit to cross it.

They are grateful for their children. Their three sons have served on missions, their four children have married in the temple. There are now twenty-seven grandchildren and eleven great-grandchildren. Like all parents, President and Sister Kimball pray constantly over their family. Conscious that each is an individual spirit, each with his agency, they are attentive and concerned as father and mother, grandfather and grandmother, and great-grandfather and great-grandmother.

Typical of the concern of Brother and Sister Kimball for their children was the challenge they faced when Eddie was stricken with polio. Their home was in Safford, Arizona. At that time the treatment available was in California. The Kimballs came to know the road between Safford and Los Angeles in intimate detail, for they drove it time after time after time. There were the operations and the trips back for checkups, for therapy. There were trips for further treatment, some of them disguised as family vacations. Always they were trying to make the best of what would come under the ordinary heading of trouble. But there were no complaints about the pressures of travel and the financial burden, for this was their boy.

President Spencer W. Kimball is a poet. His sermons, prepared with great labor, are lyrical and beautiful and powerful. Yet their power is not in their prose but in the preaching. It has been said that a poet is next to a prophet. In President Kimball we find a prophet who is a poet.

Perhaps this gift came from his illustrious grandfather, of whom it was said, "A lover of choice language, he was, and, when loftily inspired, a user of much that was beautiful and sublime. A never-failing fountain of poetic thought and imagery" (Orson F. Whitney, *Life of Heber C. Kimball* [1945], 70).

Consider a sample or two, a few nuggets only, from a gold mine of strength and power in his sermons. In a sermon on the Book of Mormon, we find this:

"Across the stage of this drama of life through the ages, marched actors in exotic, colorful costumes from the blood-painted nudity of the warrior to the lavish, ornamented pageantry of royal courts—some actors loathsome and degraded, others so near perfection that they conversed with angels and with God. There are the sowers and reapers, the artisans, the engineers, the traders, and the toilers, the rake in his debauchery, the alcoholic with his liquor, the pervert rotting in his sex, the warrior in his armor, the missionary on his knees. This dramatic story is one of the greatest ever played by man" (Conference Report, April 1963, 63).

In a sermon on tithing, these paragraphs:

"I saw him lying in his death among luxurious furnishings in a palatial home. His had been a vast estate. And I folded his arms upon his breast, and drew down the little curtains over his eyes. I spoke at his funeral, and I followed the cortege from the good piece of earth he had claimed to his grave, a tiny, oblong area the length of a tall man, the width of a heavy one.

"Yesterday I saw that same estate, yellow in grain, green in lucerne, white in cotton, seemingly unmindful of him who had claimed it. Oh, puny man, see the busy ant moving the sands of the sea" (Conference Report, April 1968, 74).

And who could forget his description of Berlin following the war:

"We went to Europe," he said, "without a camera—the only persons in Europe, I think, who did not have a camera."

And so he recorded his impressions with his pen. From his journal:

"Friday, August 26, 1955:
Ten years now since the world war tragedy!
Here were fences around the former grand estates
Wire fences,
Rusty fences,
Wind-blown rotting fences,
Proud, haughty fences leveled in humiliation.

Metal gates hanging unkept; creaking hinges.

Naked walls, irregular walls, pock-marked walls, and
    weeds growing from their toothlike stabbing jaggedness;
Green ivy trying hard to cover the nakedness of walls—
    gaping walls—absent walls but with scores of broken bricks
    still indicating where—
Chipped walls,
Grass atop the jagged walls holding brave
    little flowers struggling for existence.

There were windows, too many windows, cold, open windows,
    open to storm and sky
Boarded-up windows,
Bricked-up windows,
Glassless windows.

There were jagged chimneys piercing skies,
Iron bedsteads hanging from chimneys,
Plumbing pipes reaching into space like dragons' claws.

Here were trees—
Limbless trees except for new growth,

Tall trees leaning, branches all one side,
Amputated limbs and trunks, but not with saw.
Jagged arms pointing at—at whom are they pointing?
Vines climbing naked trunks to cover broken limbs and
*   torn and battered trees.*
Small trees, ragged shrubs growing from the rubble where
*   once were pianos, rugs and pictures;*
Trees growing untended
Vines climbing and spreading to cover ugliness.
Nature trying to sweeten sourness.
Grostesque figures standing out against the sky,
*   pointing into space like accusing hands and fingers.*
Empty pools,
Broken swimming pools, a reminder of leisure and luxury
*   of forgotten rich.*
Twisted steel,
Arches without buildings,
Doorways without walls
Porches and doorways, nothing else, porches and
*   doorways.*
Sagging floors,
Ceilings of splintered wood, shattered plaster
*   hanging like cobwebs.*

Excavations like graves,
Excavations which are graves—
Excavations where rodents play and insects find their homes.

Proud estates, quarter blocks, ghost yards, spectre houses,
*   all so still.*
Silence, silence, deathly silence
No playful shouts, no children laugh.
Silent walls, silent houses, silent blocks, silent death.
Bricks are here—

Broken bricks,
Pulverized bricks,
Piled up bricks, covering bones of humans never found.

Rubble, rubble, rubble,
Foundations up-ended,
Rotting wood,
Twisted steel,
Destruction, devastation, desolation,
Broken fountains,
Shattered statues,
Creaking shutters,
Rusty mail boxes,
Rustiness!
Ugliness!
Jaggedness!
Screaming jaggedness!

Unmolested squirrels scampering,
Tiny birds twittering

To bring back life to deadness.
Walls, chimneys, trees, grotesque writhing apparitions!
Persons? Things? Dragons? Disfigured, deformed things
Slumped in misery and shame.

(Conference Report, October 1955, 76–77)

And there are many other sermons: "Blind Obedience or Obedience of Faith," "Broken Power Lines," "Hidden Wedges," "Tragedy or Destiny"—inspiration pouring through a man with a gift and the spirit to sustain it.

Many of his sermons over the years have been about the Lamanites. A concern for them has dominated his ministry.

The Prophet Joseph Smith recorded, "The title-page of the Book of Mormon is a literal translation, taken from the very last leaf, on the left hand side of the collection or book of plates, which contained the record which has been translated. . . . Said title page is not by any means a modern composition, either of mine or of any other man who has lived or does live in this generation" *(History of The Church of Jesus Christ of Latter-day Saints,* ed. B. H. Roberts, 2d ed. rev., 7 vols. [1932–51], 1:71).

The title page declares: "Wherefore, it is an abridgment of the record of the people of Nephi, and also of the Lamanites—Written to the Lamanites, who are a remnant of the house of Israel; and also to Jew and Gentile."

No man in this dispensation has done more to see that the message of the Book of Mormon gets to the Lamanites than has Spencer W. Kimball. No man has worked with greater zeal that "they may know the covenants of the Lord, that they are not cast off forever" (Book of Mormon, title page).

There are more than 60 million people of Lamanite extraction. It is no accident that the Church now prospers among them in Mexico, Central and South America, in the islands of the sea, and among the Indian tribes of North America. President Kimball, all of his life as an Apostle, has restlessly urged and encouraged and pressed the work among them.

"I do not know when I began to love the children of Lehi. It may have come to me at birth, because those years preceding and after I was born, were spent by my father on missions among the Indians in Indian territory. He was president of the mission. This love may have come in those first years of my childhood, when my father used to sing the Indian chants to us children and show us souvenirs from and pictures of his Indian friends. It may have come from my patriarchal blessing which was given to me by Patriarch Samuel Claridge, when I was nine years of age. One line of the blessing reads: 'You will preach the gospel to many people, but more especially to the Lamanites, for the Lord will bless you with the gift of language and power to portray before that people, the gospel in great plainness. You will see them organized and be prepared to stand as the bulwark "round this people."'

"I do not know when my appreciation for them came, but I have always had a sympathetic heart for the sons and daughters of Lehi" (Conference Report, April 1947, 144).

On 13 September 1946, President Kimball recorded the following in his journal:

"I went down to the office of President George Albert Smith at his request . . . relative to the Indians. We talked about the Navajos in the mission. He then said, 'Now I want you to look after the Indians—they have been neglected. You watch all the Indians. I want you to have charge and look after all the Indians in all the world and this includes those in the Islands also.'

"I told him I would do my best. I told him that this commission, given me twice before, fulfilled my patriarchal blessing literally. . . . He indicated that he wished me to lead this committee in a vigorous program for all the Indians in all the world."

In President Kimball's mind this burden was easy and the yoke was light, for this would be a labor of love.

He has often spoken of Moroni, who wandered alone, having custody of the records prepared by his father, Mormon.

"I make not myself known to the Lamanites lest they should destroy me.

" . . . Wherefore, I wander whithersoever I can for the safety of mine own life" (Moroni 1:1, 3).

In spite of the fact that they were seeking his life, Moroni continued:

"I write a few more things, that perhaps they may be of worth unto my brethren, the Lamanites, in some future day, according to the will of the Lord" (Moroni 1:4).

There follows the only treatise in the Book of Mormon on church government. The chapters that follow explain the bestowal of the Holy Ghost, the ordination of priests and teachers, the mode of administering the sacrament, the conditions and mode of baptism, and church discipline. All of this, addressed to the Lamanites.

President Kimball has worked unceasingly and unrelentingly for them. As Moroni of old, he has sought to "cause my church to be established among them" (D&C 28:8).

As Moroni concluded his writing, he again addressed his words to the Lamanites: "Now I, Moroni, write somewhat as seemeth me good; and I write unto my brethren, the Lamanites" (Moroni 10:1).

And then comes the great declaration, applying perhaps to all, but, as most have overlooked, addressed "to the Lamanites."

"And when ye shall receive these things, I would exhort you that ye would ask God, the Eternal Father, in the name of Christ, if these things are not true; and if ye shall ask with a sincere heart, with real intent, having faith in Christ, he will manifest the truth of it unto you, by the power of the Holy Ghost.

"And by the power of the Holy Ghost ye may know the truth of all things" (Moroni 10:4–5).

If there is one golden thread characteristic of the ministry of Spencer W. Kimball, it is his love for, and his ministry among, the Lamanites.

To enter President Kimball's office is to see the mementos of his travels among them. A Sioux headdress, given when he was adopted into the tribe and given a name. The painting of a Hopi man. Another of a Chilean Indian. The wooden doll, lovingly carved and dressed by little Sister Two Dogs at Pine Ridge, South Dakota. The carved plaques of the Amazon Indians. The bow and arrow from another tribe. The beautiful carved figures of a Bolivian Indian man and woman. And mementos from the islands of the sea.

The Indian name he was given is Washte-Ho-Wamblee. The literal translation is: "Good voice eagle." And, as he was told by his Lamanite brethren, it means: He who flies across the world lifting his voice to bring good tidings of truth.

This is no ordinary man who presides over The Church of Jesus Christ of Latter-day Saints. The day he was ordained an Apostle he became a different man, a special witness of the Lord Jesus Christ like those in ancient times.

"He went out into a mountain to pray, and continued all night in prayer to God.

"And when it was day, he called unto him his disciples: and of them he chose twelve, whom also he named apostles" (Luke 6:12–13).

In that day He called them: Peter, James, John, Andrew, Philip, Bartholomew, and the others, to stand as special witnesses of Him.

In this day He has called them: Spencer, Nathan, Marion, Ezra, Mark, Delbert, and the others—Apostles of the Lord Jesus Christ. Men possessing the same authority, sustained by the same witness as those He ordained in former days.

The Lord Himself is the head of His Church. Spencer W. Kimball, a prophet, seer and revelator, is its President. As one among those who know him very well and who love him very much, as one who shares in that special witness, I testify to that.

26

EZRA TAFT BENSON: WE HONOR NOW HIS JOURNEY

I'm grateful for the spirit of peace that is here on this sacred occasion as we bid farewell to our beloved President. Forty-six years ago, in Brigham City, Elder Ezra Taft Benson ordained me a Seventy. My next meeting with him was twelve years later in Washington, D.C. A. Theodore Tuttle and I, then supervisors of seminary, were there on Church school business, and he invited us to lunch with him at his office in the Department of Agriculture. As he fed us, in return, we quenched his thirst for news about the Church.

Those were the years he served in government, meeting the great men of the world: Chiang Kai-shek, Khrushchev, Ben-Gurion, the shah of Iran, Tito, Eisenhower.

Whether entertained in an ordinary hotel or the lavish palace of the Peacock Throne, he would say, "This is too good for a farm boy from Idaho."

But you cannot find Ezra Taft Benson in those government years.

From an address given at the funeral services for President Ezra Taft Benson; see *Ensign*, July 1994, 32–34.

He must be measured by the teachings of the book that dominated his thoughts, controlled his conduct, and inspired his very soul: the Book of Mormon: Another Testament of Jesus Christ.

In the pages of the Book of Mormon, President Benson found the focus of his service.

The prophet Nephi, who faithfully kept a secular history on large plates, was commanded to keep another account: this time, a record of the ministry—the small plates of Nephi.

His brother Jacob wrote that when Nephi gave the records to him, "he gave me, Jacob, a commandment that I should write upon these [small] plates a few of the things which I considered to be *most precious; that I should not touch, save it were lightly,* concerning the *history* of this people. . . .

"And if there were *preaching which was sacred,* or *revelation which was great,* or *prophesying,* that I should engraven . . . them upon these plates, and touch upon *them* as *much* as it were possible, *for Christ's sake,* and for the sake of our people" (Jacob 1:2, 4; italics added).

"Wherefore, the things which are pleasing unto the world I do *not* write, but the things which are pleasing unto God [I write]" (1 Nephi 6:5; italics added).

"And upon these [small plates] I write *the things of my soul,* and many of the *scriptures* which are engraven upon the plates of brass. For *my soul delighteth in the scriptures,* and my heart pondereth them, and writeth them for the learning and the profit of my children" (2 Nephi 4:15; italics added).

President Benson had the kind of honesty that made people shake their heads and the kind of courage that made him essentially immune to criticism or opposition.

Opposition

He learned about opposition as a missionary boy in England. An angry mob separated him from his companion. They fled for their very lives. How they rejoiced when they found each other to be safe.

He always kept this verse from the Book of Mormon in his wallet: "No weapon that is formed against thee shall prosper; and every tongue that shall revile against thee in judgment thou shalt condemn. This is the heritage of the servants of the Lord, and their righteousness is of me, saith the Lord" (3 Nephi 22:17).

And always this statement was kept on his desk or in his study: "Be right, and then be easy to live with, if possible, but in that order."

He was like the Old Testament prophet Nehemiah who rallied the people of Jerusalem to build a wall about the city. The enemies ridiculed their efforts, saying, "That which they build, if a fox go up, he shall even break down their stone wall" (Nehemiah 4:3).

"Nevertheless [he] made [a] prayer unto our God, and set a watch against them day and night" (Nehemiah 4:9).

The enemies sent word, "saying, Come, let us meet together . . . in the plain of Ono. But they thought to do [him] mischief.

"And [he] sent messengers unto them, saying, I am doing a great work, so that I cannot come down: why should the work cease, whilst I leave it, and come down to you?" (Nehemiah 6:2–3).

President Benson had a great work to do, a great ministry to perform. He reminded us always that "the gospel can only prosper in an atmosphere of freedom."

He had unlimited faith in people, for he had read in the Book of Mormon, "It is not common that the voice of the people desireth anything contrary to that which is right; but it is common for the lesser part of the people to desire that which is not right; therefore this shall ye observe and make it your law—to do your business by the voice of the people" (Mosiah 29:26).

And as a prophet he warned us of the verse that followed: "And if the time comes that the voice of the people doth choose iniquity, then is the time that the judgments of God will come upon you; yea, then is the time he will visit you with great destruction even as he has hitherto visited this land" (Mosiah 29:27).

How many times have we heard him measure decisions, asking, "What's best for the kingdom?"

How many times has he told us, "It's the Spirit that counts"?

Music

President Benson loved good music of all kinds. He taught that the hymns of the Restoration were the language of the Spirit; that the quiet hymns and the exalted anthems will whisper to the soul words that are felt rather than heard.

He learned to sing them from his father as they milked cows. He learned them by watching his mother as she would spread newspapers on the floor near the coal stove, set up the ironing board, and put the flatirons made of cast iron on the stove to heat. Then, as she carefully ironed the white temple clothing, she would invite the spirit of contentment, of inspiration, of revelation by singing softly the hymns of the Restoration.

We honor now the journey of ninety-four years.

A leader we both knew well and loved dearly, President Joseph Fielding Smith, wrote these lines about the journey of life:

> *Does the journey seem long,*
> *The path rugged and steep?*
> *Are there briars and thorns on the way?*
> *Do sharp stones cut your feet*
> *As you struggle to rise*
> *To the heights through the heat of the day?*
>
> *Is your heart faint and sad,*
> *Your soul weary within,*

As you toil 'neath your burden of care?
Does the load heavy seem
You are forced now to lift?
Is there no one your burden to share?

Are you weighed down with grief,
Is there pain in your breast,
As you wearily journey along?
Are you looking behind
To the valley below?
Do you wish you were back in the throng?

Let your heart be not faint
Now the journey's begun;
There is One who still beckons to you.
Look upward in gladness
And take hold of his hand,
He will lead you to heights that are new.

A land holy and pure
Where all trouble doth end,
And your life shall be free from all sin,
Where no tears shall be shed
For no sorrows remain;
Take his hand and with him enter in.

(*Hymns* [1948], no. 245)

Now this dear, venerable prophet has entered in, there to rejoice with his beloved Flora and to speak of their wonderful family, there to rejoice with Joseph and Brigham and John and Wilford and the others.

The prophets who preceded him, ancient and modern, have on occasion communed with the servants of the Lord on this earth. So it well may be that we have not seen the last of this great prophet of God.

I testify that the veil between this mortal realm and the spirit world opens to such revelation and visitation as the needs of the Church and kingdom of God on earth may require. I bear witness that he was a prophet of God; that Jesus is the Christ, the Son of God; that the gospel of Jesus Christ is true; and that this true servant now takes His hand and enters in.

27

HOWARD W. HUNTER: HE ENDURED TO THE END

Friday morning President Gordon B. Hinckley called and said quietly, "The President just died; will you notify the Twelve?" I said to myself, "Well, he endured to the very end." And *endure is* the word to describe him.

I looked up the word *endure* in the dictionary. To my surprise it means "to last, to suffer continuously." That is exactly what he did; he lasted, and he suffered continually, and he did endure.

A Lesson

There is much to be learned from the very brief administration of President Howard W. Hunter. The condition of his health and the very brevity of his administration, only nine months, provide the lesson. The lesson centers in President Howard W. Hunter himself!

Dr. J. Poulson Hunter attended the President for thirty years.

From an address given at the funeral services for President Howard W. Hunter; see *Ensign*, April 1995, 28–30.

He reminded me of an orchestra leader, directing teams of specialists called to treat one condition or another.

Several years ago after President Hunter had been released from the hospital for the second time in a few months, this wise and experienced physician said to me in confidence, "My experience tells me that when a man of his age experiences two assaults of the magnitude that he has suffered during a year, he will not survive the third one." In a matter of weeks the third strike came—the President went down again, but he was not out.

I once asked President Hunter if he had a doctor's book, and if so I wanted to borrow it. He asked why. I said, "I want to keep it. It seems to me you read through it looking for some major affliction you haven't had, wonder what it would be like, and decide to try it."

When he was unable to walk or even stand, arrangements were made for him to speak in general conference from a sitting position. He quipped to the congregation, "You seem to enjoy conference so much sitting down, I thought I would do the same."

After many months of agonizing therapy, with tender encouragement and help from Dale Springer, his loved and trusted aide, he was able to stand at the pulpit to speak. He lost his balance and fell over backward. We helped him up. He matter-of-factly continued his speech without missing a word. There was but a moment's interruption. The television audience did not even know he had fallen. He had broken three ribs in that fall.

We accompanied him to Jerusalem for the dedication of the BYU Center. As I was speaking, there was some excitement in the back of the hall. Men in military uniforms had entered the room. They sent a note to President Hunter. I turned and asked for instructions. He said, "There's been a bomb threat. Are you afraid?" I said, "No." He said, "Neither am I; finish your talk."

Later at BYU there was that other incident. He was confronted with what was apparently a bomb. He said nothing, just stood and looked on as if to say, "When you are through, I'd like to go on with my talk." And so he did.

Recently I asked if he was in any pain. He said, "No." I said, "Would you tell us if you were?" and he smiled. When it came to pain, he was a very private man. It is not an easy thing to grow old on stage.

Now, these are but a few samples of the problems President Hunter endured. And I speak of them for a purpose. There is a message to future generations in what he did and what he was.

There are those who wonder at the system where the senior Apostle, invariably now an older man, becomes the President of the Church.

Those who do not understand write to us or publish articles saying, "Isn't it time now to do the sensible thing and install a vigorous, young leader to face the challenge of a growing international Church?"

They fail to see the divine inspiration in the system established by the Lord. Granted, it does not work as the wisdom of men would dictate. The Lord reminded Isaiah:

"My thoughts are not your thoughts, neither are your ways my ways. . . . For as the heavens are higher than the earth, so are my ways higher than your ways, and my thoughts than your thoughts" (Isaiah 55:8–9).

See what the Lord has provided. Nowhere on this earth is there a body of men of leadership and authority as completely devoid of aspiring. The very system that seems so strange to many just does not allow it; neither would the Lord permit it. There is no jockeying for position or power, no soliciting for votes, no hint of cultivating influence in any self-serving way.

There is a brotherhood that accommodates differing views and personalities, but we are *one*. The authority in the administration of the Church is independent of any individual and is held in trust by fifteen men who have been ordained as Apostles. President Hunter's life has taught us that regardless of the age or infirmity of any man among them, including the President, the work goes on.

He said to the Church, "My walk is slower now, but my spirit is young and my mind is clear," and in these last few weeks he had a clarity of mind and a quickness of response that astonished those who knew him best.

The brief administration of President Howard W. Hunter symbolizes the supernal spiritual genius in the organization which the Lord has revealed. It is a testimony that this is the Church of Jesus Christ and that He presides over it. The Lord has his own measure of the credentials of one who will lead this Church.

When Samuel was sent to choose the prophet to succeed himself, the Lord said, "Look not on his countenance, or on the height of his stature; . . . for the Lord seeth not as man seeth; for man looketh on the outward appearance, but the Lord looketh on the heart" (1 Samuel 16:7).

Paul said, "The natural man receiveth not the things of the Spirit of God: for they are foolishness unto him: neither can he know them, because they are spiritually discerned" (1 Corinthians 2:14).

If you look through the lens of your natural eyes only, you will not see the genius in the system that not only allows for but is blessed by a President Howard W. Hunter, whose age and infirmity were really irrelevant.

Travel and Experience

No man comes to be President of this Church except he has been apprenticed for a lifetime. In association with his Brethren who hold the keys, he has participated in decisions and faced every problem. President Hunter walked for more than thirty years with LeGrand Richards, who remembered Wilford Woodruff; and Joseph Anderson, who died at a hundred and two and came to his assignment as replacement for a man hired by Brigham Young.

No Self-Serving Thought

What man with the experience and consecration and age of President Howard W. Hunter would pay any attention to popularity or power or pain—or would even think, much less act, in any way that would be self-serving?

He does not become President of the Church without knowing the Church all across the world. Notwithstanding his physical frailty, President Hunter has been an unrelenting traveler. Just in the past very few years, I myself have traveled with him to South America, to Africa, to Europe three times, to Israel, to Asia, to Hong Kong, and into China. Just six months ago we followed him in cable cars up Jungfrau, in the Swiss Alps, and by cog rail up the Matterhorn itself. And I am only one of the Twelve.

President Hunter, as with those who preceded him and those who will follow him, came to that office with a preparation and a purification that the world cannot understand. Each comes to that office attended by "the Spirit of truth; whom the world cannot receive, because it seeth him not, neither knoweth him," and they have the trust and the promise of the Lord: "I will not leave you comfortless: I will come to you" (John 14:17–18).

The administration of President Howard W. Hunter, though very brief, has been a historic one. Things have transpired during those few months of his leadership, some of them as yet unannounced, which will bless this Church for generations to come.

Forgive me for having avoided personal references to my beloved friend. President Hinckley reminded us once that "tears come easily to old men." President Hunter knew that Donna and I loved him, and we know that that love was returned.

Three days before President Hunter's passing, Elder Russell M. Nelson and I visited with the President. He was seated in the sun room which overlooks the temple and the gardens. We knelt before him, each holding one of his hands. As we talked with him, he kept looking over his shoulder into the living room and then called to his wife, Inis.

Ever present and ever attentive, she responded immediately and asked what he needed. He said, "You are too far away; I want you close to me." I said, "President, she was only thirty feet away." He said, "I know; that's too far."

Of the many verses that teach what enduring means, I will share but one: "Blessed are they who shall seek to bring forth my Zion at that day, for they shall have the gift and the power of the Holy Ghost; and if they endure unto the end they shall be lifted up at the last day, and shall be saved in the everlasting kingdom of the Lamb; and whoso shall publish peace, yea, tidings of great joy, how beautiful upon the mountains shall they be" (1 Nephi 13:37).

Surely President Hunter endured to the end.

"Precious in the sight of the Lord is the death of his saints" (Psalm 116:15).

"Wherefore, fear not even unto death; for in this world your joy is not full, but in me your joy is full" (D&C 101:36).

I bear witness that we have had the association of a holy man, a prophet of God, a beloved friend, our President.

28

GORDON B. HINCKLEY: THIS GENTLE PROPHET

I first met Gordon B. Hinckley more than fifty years ago. I was called as an Assistant to the Twelve in the same conference he was sustained as a member of the Quorum of the Twelve Apostles.

His first words at the pulpit when he was sustained as an Assistant to the Twelve were: "I know that I have not come that road alone, and I feel very grateful for the many men and women—the great and good men who are here today, and the ... wonderful people, many of whose names I do not remember—who have helped me" (Conference Report, Apr. 1958, 123).

Gordon B. Hinckley first arrived at Church headquarters on his way home from his mission in England. He had been asked by the mission president to report to the First Presidency: Presidents Heber J. Grant, J. Reuben Clark Jr., and David O. McKay. The fifteen-minute meeting lasted over an hour. He was asked to serve as secretary to the new Church mission literature committee.

From an address given at the funeral services for President Gordon B. Hinckley; see *Ensign*, March 2008, 24–26.

He was on his own to rustle around to find an empty office somewhere. A friend, whose father owned an office supply store, gave him an old, warped table. He put a block of wood under one short leg. He brought his own typewriter from home.

He went to the supply room for a ream of paper and was asked, "Do you have any idea how many sheets of paper are in a ream?"

He replied, "Yes, five hundred sheets."

"What in the world are you going to do with five hundred sheets of paper?"

He answered, "I am going to write on them one sheet at a time."

He never stopped writing. For years I have had a weekly meeting with President Hinckley. Often I found him at his desk writing out his talks in longhand.

My first assignment as an Assistant to the Twelve was as assistant to President Hinckley in the Missionary Department.

Soon thereafter he left to tour the missions in Europe with President Henry D. Moyle. After he returned, he told me that one of the hardest things he ever had to do happened in Düsseldorf.

On their last evening in Europe, President Moyle hosted a dinner for the missionaries, including President Hinckley's son Richard. President Hinckley said good-bye to his son at the hotel. He said that to watch Richard walk away with his companion into the cold, dark night was the hardest thing he ever had to do. He wept as he told me about it.

President Hinckley's extraordinary intelligence and his incredible memory were immediately apparent. But I had learned something else more important. I had seen inside of President Gordon B. Hinckley. He has always been a very private person, and only occasionally does one see inside of him.

In trying to describe President Hinckley's ability to communicate, I recalled years ago traveling in Pakistan with Elder Jacob de Jager, one of the Seventy, whom we referred to as "the smiling, happy Dutchman."

Our host was Mr. Suleman Habib, a longtime friend from a prominent banking family in Karachi.

One day Suleman took us out of the city into the countryside to see one of his farms. We came upon a large group of laborers, poorly dressed, building a road with pick and shovel. They spoke in Urdu, a language neither Jacob nor I had ever heard before. The car had hardly stopped when Jacob was out the door. He mingled with the laborers.

Suleman watched him intently and then turned to me and said, "That man can communicate with these Urdu people better than I can." And a moment later he added, "That man could charm a donkey or a king!"

Whatever power of communication and charm Suleman saw in Jacob de Jager was found in rich measure in Gordon B. Hinckley.

There came to my office one day an Islamic cleric who was in Salt Lake City to receive treatment at the Moran Eye Center. I arranged for an audience with the First Presidency. Dr. Abdurrahman Wahid, much like President Hinckley, had a sparkling sense of humor. Accompanying Dr. Wahid was Dr. Alwi Shihab, a professor of Islamic studies at Harvard University.

In that meeting, Dr. Wahid mentioned that he had been asked to run for the office of president of Indonesia. "If I am elected," Dr. Wahid said, "Alwi Shihab will be my foreign minister."

President Hinckley said, "If you decide to run and you are elected, I will come and visit you in Jakarta."

He was elected, and we did go to Jakarta, where President Hinckley was the guest of honor at a dinner given at the presidential palace.

The first message of condolence I received on the death of President Hinckley was from Alwi Shihab. Yesterday there arrived a very large floral tribute from President Wahid, former president of Indonesia.

I have regarded this power of communication and charm in President Hinckley as brotherly love and humility. It was always apparent whether he was with the laborers on a dusty road or a banquet in a presidential palace.

President Hinckley grew up schooled in the doctrines of the gospel. His roots go back to Cove Fort, in central Utah. Restored, it stands now much as it did in the pioneer days when his grandfather built it.

Much of President Hinckley's growth I attribute to his wife, Marjorie Pay Hinckley, who was patient with a man who was always on the go, always ten steps ahead of her. For example, one evening he was packing for an overseas trip the following morning.

Marjorie asked, "Well, am I going to go with you?"

He responded, "We don't have to decide that right now!"

He knew, as we all should know, that the doctrines of Jesus Christ are synonymous with family.

Succession to the presidency of The Church of Jesus Christ of Latter-day Saints is a remarkable process. Always the senior Apostle becomes the President, and the next senior becomes the President of the Quorum of the Twelve Apostles. Outlined in the revelations are the truths and instructions by which the Brethren administer the Church. Whatever the crisis or whatever the opportunity, the directions and guidance can be found in the verses of scripture.

No one who has known the order of things speculates on who will be the next President of the Church. It has always been this pattern. There is no aspiring for the position, no avoiding the Lord's will.

Gordon B. Hinckley did not seek the many calls and assignments that came to him, but he did not shy away either.

In one of the earliest revelations, the Lord said, "That every man might speak in the name of God the Lord, even the Savior of the world" (D&C 1:20) that "the weak things of the world shall come forth and break down the mighty and strong ones" (D&C 1:19).

With the Church growing very rapidly worldwide, we often go to distant places to organize or reorganize a unit of the Church. We are sometimes asked, "Where on earth will you find the new leaders?" We do not have to find them. They are already there, just as Gordon B. Hinckley was there. The Lord provides them. They are serving faithfully and paying for the privilege in tithes and offerings.

In a separate ordinance following baptism, members of the Church have conferred upon them the Holy Ghost, which the scriptures explain will "teach you all things, and bring all things to your remembrance" (John 14:26). The Holy Ghost is the Inspirer. Inspiration is always there, if you learn to live with it and for it.

One of the things that President Hinckley understood best is the word *family*. It is not difficult to find statements on the family in his sermons and talks and counsel, whether to large congregations, to individuals, or more particularly to families.

I pay tribute to the family of Gordon Bitner and Marjorie Pay Hinckley. They can be described as ideal. They, like their father, are unassuming. Whatever prominence that has come to them does not show any more than it was visible in him.

In the cemetery not too far from here, there is a headstone with "Marjorie Pay Hinckley" engraved on it and, beside her name, the name of "Gordon Bitner Hinckley."

When Mary approached the tomb of Jesus, an angel said, "He is not here: for he is risen" (Matthew 28:6; see also Mark 16:6; Luke 24:6).

In due course it can be said of Gordon Bitner and Marjorie Pay Hinckley, "They are not here, for they are risen and together."

May our Father bless the memory of this gentle prophet and his eternal companion and the sacred work over which he presided.

INDEX

Aaronic Priesthood: restored by John
the Baptist, 13, 19–21; as preparatory priesthood, 81–83; bishop responsible for members of, 89
Adversary: inspires to evil, 21, 115; has
no body, 113; angels of, 159, 173,
189; rebellion of, 187; beguiling of
Eve by, 188; power of, 191, 224
Alcott, Louisa May, "My Little
Kingdom," 56
"All the Water in the World," 54–55
Anderson, Joseph, 245
Angel(s): ministering of, 19, 176; speak
by power of Holy Ghost, 20, 180,
194; speaking with tongues of, 20,
41; visitation to Alma, 50; and conscience, 154; of the adversary, 159,
173, 189; and gifts of the Spirit,
165; appear by faith, 176; office of,
177; sent to Adam, 188

Apostasy: Dark Ages of, 18, 156; and
priesthood authority, 156
Apostle(s): office of, restored by Peter,
James, and John, 19; arrest of, 32;
ordination of, 100; teachings of,
hard to bear, 206; ancient and modern, 235; authority held in trust by,
244; senior member of, 244, 251
Atonement of Jesus Christ: offers redemption from spiritual death, 10,
188; as ever-present power, 10–12,
13; healing power of, 11, 117;
activated daily with prayer, 12; in
hymns, 24; in Restoration scripture,
29; bishops to teach of, 90; Book of
Mormon testifies of, 94; as vicarious
ordinance, 218; temple work as visible testimony of, 219

Bangerter, Wm. Grant, 207
Baptism: unto repentance, 18, 19–20;

253